# TRULY HUMAN

## Recovering Your Humanity
## in a Broken World

KEVIN SCHERER

ANCIENT FAITH PUBLISHING
CHESTERTON, INDIANA

Published by:
  Ancient Faith Publishing
  A Division of Ancient Faith Ministries
  P.O. Box 748
  Chesterton, IN 46304

Unless otherwise noted, Scripture quotations are taken from the New King James Version, © 1979, 1980, 1982 by Thomas Nelson, Inc. Used by permission.

Cover photo collage: Sky and man photo from Shutterstock ©Stefano Garau; Constellation hands from Wallup.net.

ISBN: 978-1-944967-05-5

Printed in the United States of America

*To my daughters:*
*Hannah, Julia, Clare, Audrey, and Claire.*
*I pray this book will help you discern the path of genuine*
*freedom and fulfillment in your lives.*

# Contents

# Foreword

In chapter 10 of Kevin Scherer's marvelous book, *Truly Human*, he shares with the reader a vulnerable admission that follows on the train of many pages about the journey of faith: "As I write this book, I'm barely recovering from three devastating years. My ex-wife and I divorced after twenty-two years of marriage, I lost my job, my pastoral vocation, was forced to move away from my three beautiful girls to find work, foreclosed on a house, filed bankruptcy, was forced to say goodbye to a woman I deeply loved, and lost my precious mother to a painful disease."

When first reading Kevin's book, I considered recommending that he bring this confession to the front of the work. I think it's important that readers know that when Kevin speaks about the brokenness of humanity and the journey toward wholeness, he speaks from a place of his own very deep and personal experiences of brokenness and the hard work of repentance, self-examination, and struggle to become truly human. Yet I understand why he reserves this confession for the very end. Thus, if there is no clear way for Kevin to bring this to the reader up front, I will.

I first met Kevin in a time of my own brokenness. I speak about this in the film *Becoming Truly Human*, which shares my journey from religious non-affiliation to Eastern Orthodox Christianity. The journey I share in the film is less a journey toward wholeness and more a journey to the road that leads to wholeness. In my recounting of the catalytic events that propelled me and my family into the Orthodox Church, I speak about my life crashing down in the course of only months. In this very short period of time, we completed our adoption of a special needs child, a close family member attempted suicide, and I was diagnosed with cancer.

In that film, I recount the self-examination that this series of events prompted in me with the brief statement, "There were all sorts of issues in my own life that I wished I had talked with [my wife] Heather about. That was such a jarring experience for me that I finally did do the scariest thing possible and say, Here's all the stuff."

That vague gloss—a gloss intended to offer to the audience no more than was needed for the story—represents a time of deep trauma, trauma unlike anything I have ever experienced before or since. It was a time when all I had built, every piece of my carefully crafted façade, was torn down by the brutality of the death that entered the world through sin. And it was in the face of seeing that façade crumble that I entered into my own journey of authentic repentance, self-examination, and struggle to become truly human. It was in the midst of that that I met Kevin, who would eventually become my godfather.

I must confess that my journey toward Orthodoxy was one

that involved years of study—a fact recounted in *Becoming Truly Human*. Yet, if I'm honest with myself and with readers, the lion's share of those years was a journey of the intellect. Not until my life fell apart did I begin to learn a very important truth about Christianity as understood in the Eastern Church.

Theology is ultimately a way of life. The theologian is not the one who reads and studies; the theologian is the one who prays. As my life unraveled in my hands, what I did not realize was that I was only then beginning a journey from the threshold of theology to true theology. Only then did I begin to see that, as beautiful as the teachings of the Eastern Church are (and they are filled with Beauty), they exist in order to direct humanity toward life. These teachings exist to show us how to claw our way out of the grave and find what we most deeply desire but vainly chase after in pursuits that can never deliver. It was at this threshold—the threshold of true theology—that I first met Kevin.

Our journeys are not so different, largely because our failings are not so different. And even more so, the roots of those failings—the very real brokenness, or better the death at work in our members—may well be the very same. I was able to share with Kevin in painful transparency all that had transpired in my life outwardly. But more than that, I was able to lay before him my inner life, my brokenness, and the fears and hurts I had kept hidden, lest I utter them aloud to another human being—as if their mere utterance would make them somehow more real. Yet, when I finished baring my soul, I found that Kevin understood. He offered to me in reply the greatest gift he could—love, mercy, compassion, understanding, and truth. He offered to me his own story and what he had learned from it. And beyond this, he offered me himself, a companion on the road ahead whenever one may be needed. I don't know if I fully appreciated at the time what a gift that is. But I do now.

Since that time Kevin has become a dear friend and mentor. I have learned that I can bring to him my fears, troubles, patterns of thought, really anything from my inner world. And what I can be confident of is that I will be met with both love and honesty. Kevin is gifted at cutting through delusions and self-deception with truth, wisdom, and candor, offering light in dark places. I'm grateful for him and for his friendship. I truly rely on his gifts for the road ahead. And I'm delighted to say that after reading the whole of his manuscript, I can see that he has here offered to as many as would read it the same truth, wisdom, candor, and vulnerable honesty that I have come to expect from Kevin and to so deeply value.

*Truly Human* should not be taken lightly. I admit my worry that the superficial reader will too quickly pass over the gifts offered in this book. Perhaps seeing truths that appear basic on first blush—the Fall of man, the Incarnation of the Son of God, the redemption of humanity—some readers may be tempted to turn their noses up, believing they have heard all this before. But this would be a mistake.

My favorite feature of this book is Kevin's ability to begin with the familiar and somehow make it unfamiliar. His stories often draw from his experiences with events that all readers know. For example, he recounts his experiences with 9/11, an event we all have experiences with. Yet, as familiar as this event is, one quickly discovers that there is something unfamiliar about Kevin's recounting of it.

Kevin served on the ground during 9/11 as a chaplain. In this capacity, his experience of the event was unlike that of emergency response personnel or victims or onlookers. It was truly unique. Hearing his experience brings an unexpected unfamiliarity to an event that is tremendously familiar. Yet it is not only Kevin's personal stories that display this character. I find this same trait in his recounting of biblical and theological truths. While he begins with stories that are all too familiar—creation, Eden, the Incarnation—I soon find myself in a place that is unfamiliar in the best possible way.

The careful reader who gives Kevin's work the attention it deserves will find that *Truly Human* is a wonderfully personal work. Kevin draws consistently from his own journey and stories of trauma or encounter or insight. Each of these is a gift to the reader. I know from experience that it is no small thing to put oneself and one's experiences into the public sphere for scrutiny and criticism. These stories that Kevin shares are not mere sermon illustrations or anecdotes; they are deeply personal experiences that offer an insight into the human soul.

If one walks with Kevin through these, before he knows it, he will find himself hearing biblical and theological truths. Placed in the context of Kevin's own story, these truths that may be stale from overfamiliarity become animated in the truest sense. That is, these truths become filled with life, or soul (*anime*), as they are tied to Kevin's deeply personal experiences of the human condition. Yet, and as no surprise for me as one who knows him, woven throughout these truths are also tools—secular tools, if they are rightly labeled such—of self-examination and healing. But in Kevin's hands, these tools become instruments for more than mere mental health or social well-being; they are instruments for the formation of our humanity, complementing rather than competing with those gifts of the Church that aim at the undoing of death and instilling of life.

Kevin offers no clichés of human experience. For those willing to journey with him, they will find that he does not offer to the reader easy or quick solutions, as if the human condition required only a single step to the safe side of a line that divides heaven from hell. Instead, what I read in Kevin's words is something that I only came to understand and accept through the Eastern Church fathers: Spirituality is fluid.

When men turn from God, they don't become all bad, and just because a person re-turns to God doesn't make him whole. By degrees we slip into death, and by degrees we claw our way out of the grave. No single prayer nor ritual nor moment in itself can fix us. Virtue is not obtained in a moment. Each step is only one in a lifelong journey of turning and re-turning to God again and again through the hard work of honest self-examination, correction of thought, and rejection of the false foods we trade for the only life-sustaining food there is, the immortal life of God. For all else is counterfeit.

I commend Kevin for his vulnerability in sharing with readers so much of his personal life. I know it is not easy to place one's own journey in the open air for scrutiny by the broader world. Yet I hope that readers recognize the gift this is and do not treat it flippantly. Instead, I urge readers to accept the guidance here offered by one who knows deeply the brokenness of humanity and the transformative effects of a re-turn to God through the redemptive work of Christ.

Nathan A. Jacobs, Ph.D.
Visiting Scholar of Philosophy, University of Kentucky

# Acknowledgments

Frst and foremost, I want to thank my dear friend Terry for financing the writing of this book. Terry is the older brother I never had and could never deserve. Without his sacrificial contribution and weekly encouragement, this book would still be just a dream. It's my hope that his endless generosity will continue touching lives through this book.

This entire book is a footnote to what I learned at seminary from two men. The initial inspiration came from a series of lectures on St. Maximus the Confessor given by my patristics professor, John Behr. His classes were so profound that I bound all my notes. I refer to these more regularly than any book I own besides the Scriptures. The other ninety percent I owe to my seminary dean, professor, and friend, Fr. Thomas Hopko of blessed memory. I wrote this book because he didn't. And because of that, it could be so much more. His teaching, counsel, and friendship have been the holy cairns in my life.

Early on I pridefully assumed this book would be easy to write. It proved to be anything but. When I needed it most, several of my friends helped me carry this project across the finish line. Jenny Schroedel edited the first draft and mentored me through the entire process with angelic grace. Nathan Jacobs helped me reshape my approach in chapter five. And Patrick Jackson, Jordan Henderson, Jim Coles, Paul Schroeder, and Fred Arzola read my first draft and provided me with invaluable structural and content critique.

I also want to thank my pastor, Fr. John Atchison, and the members of the adult Sunday school class, who graciously allowed me to teach through the contents of this book. I hope you will recognize your influence.

Finally, I want to thank my mother for leaving me with the enduring conviction of God's immeasurable and unfailing love. Her unceasing prayers are the constant comfort of my life.

# For the Next Generation

*If we find ourselves with a desire that nothing in this world can
satisfy, the most probable explanation is that we were made for
another world.*

—C.S. Lewis[1]

I'LL NEVER FORGET THE FEELING OF RELIEF I felt the day I
heard our seminary dean and professor, Fr. Tom Hopko, tell
a group of us married seminarians that our job as parents was
not to be perfect, but to make it better for our kids than it was
for us. At the time, I had two little girls. One was three, and
the other just a few months old. It made immediate sense to me,
and, more importantly, it seemed doable. I remember thinking
to myself, if every subsequent generation in my family could be
successful at this one goal, we could create a family tree that all
of us would look at with fondness and pride. Today, I have five
girls, and their well-being and happiness mean everything to me.

My childhood wasn't awful, but it was challenging enough
that I knew exactly what I wanted to do differently. In some
ways, I think I've been successful. However, with time and a

substantial amount of failure, I've come to realize, it's easier said than done. I'm divorced now, and my children have endured their own emotional pain and anxiety. I look back and know they grew up with a father who was too often grumpy, demanding, and controlling. With time they will come to the realization that their father didn't love them perfectly, and that epiphany may come with painful memories and emotions. This book was written primarily for them—to help them make sense of and redeem the broken inheritance every human being receives from their parents. Humanity is a mysterious gift, and this book is a user's manual of sorts.

Each of us is born into this world with an instinctive desire to find meaning and purpose in our lives. Human beings have a normal and insatiable thirst to find *true north*. By nature, our lives spin obsessively until they find the course heading they were designed for. In this book, you will discover that buried beneath the surface of your personality is an even more fundamental identity—your true human nature. This God-given nature is designed with a remarkable magnetism for real freedom, fulfillment, and relational connectedness. When you have made this discovery, I will challenge you to let go of the slavery associated with creating and maintaining an acceptable, but false, social identity and embrace the freedom of your true identity in Christ.

In this book, we will explore what it means to be human and why you exist. You should expect that God will speak to you about your purpose and destiny in life. He will show you what it means to be truly human and will reveal a path that can bring your life deep fulfillment, peace, and joy. He will ask you, however, to be honest with yourself. He will ask you to consider what you really want and whether you really want to act human.

While most of the intellectual content in this book I learned in seminary, the Christian understanding of what it means to become truly human has been made clear to me experientially through the people, stories, and life experiences recounted in the following pages. Together they form a unique and ongoing revelation of God's unconditional love in my life. I hope you will learn to pay attention; God is revealing the same storyline in your life as well.

My favorite story is from one of the ancient Christian communities of the Egyptian desert. The story surrounds the interaction between a Christian monk named Lot and a spiritual elder named Joseph. Lot traveled to see the famed Joseph and to seek guidance for his Christian life. With humility, he explained to the elder his regular spiritual disciplines and way of life. "What else can I do?" he asked. "Then the old man [Joseph] stood up and stretched his hands toward heaven. His fingers became like ten lamps of fire and he said to [Lot], 'If you will, you can become all flame.'"

Make a commitment to yourself and God, now, to be brutally honest and open to new truths and personal change. With this kind of vulnerability your life can become a living flame of God's love. May God bless the journey ahead of you!

# CHAPTER ONE

# Life in the Garden

*Earth's crammed with heaven . . .*

—Elizabeth Barrett Browning[2]

O N SATURDAY NIGHT, September 15, 2001, just four days after the attack on the World Trade Center towers, I stood expressionless in front of a burning heap of rubble at Ground Zero. My mind was numb from the images, experiences, and conversations of the day. It was a chilly night, and I could see my breath in the light of the bonfire blazing in front of me. "How can this be?" I thought to myself, trying to wrap my mind and emotions around the unthinkable. I was close enough to the fire that I could feel the heat on my face. I could feel the burning anger and hatred of this event—the hatred of the terrorists and the bitterness of the American public.

All day I walked around "the Pit" as a visible member of the chaplaincy, hoping to bring the presence and comfort of God into this hole of hell. A thick, grayish-white layer of dust covered the ground and filled the air. The scene looked and felt apocalyptic. Soldiers, EMS workers, and search dogs roamed the streets, and skyscrapers lay toppled in rubble at my feet. Everywhere there were shreds of memories from the real, everyday lives of people—business reports, memos, notes on scraps of paper, and the mangled beeswax candles from a church that lay buried. Some people ran up to me panicked, asking for my prayers, while others voluntarily confessed the sins of their past. I watched one solemn procession after another of body bags being silently and reverently carried out of the Pit to a makeshift morgue.

The morgue was an open-air canopy over a temporary table, with a refrigerated eighteen-wheeler behind it. Firefighters and law enforcement officers, like pallbearers, gently lifted the bags onto the table and unzipped them. Large, burly men, tempered by years of images and experiences on the job, visibly struggled and fought back tears as the chaplain on shift said a prayer or blessing over the remains. And then, as though it were being carted into oblivion, the bag was slowly zipped back up and carried to the cold storage of a dark, cavernous truck.

All of these images haunted me as I stood paralyzed in front of the bonfire from hell. I felt alone and targeted. First responders wanted to know where God was and why He had allowed this to happen. I wondered if my presence was really a comfort, or if it was a reminder of God's absence and indifference. But through it all, I sensed His presence. And in that moment, when it seemed like hell was howling all around me, a quiet awareness fell over my heart: this burning heap in front of me was not only the result of a singular terrorist action—it was the accumulation of centuries of human greed, power, and self-absorption.

This event was not just historic, it was cosmic. This time, the cumulative weight of humanity's distortion exploded in a way that couldn't be hidden in the columns of a newspaper. All of us were forced to stare evil in the face. And as I did, I saw myself. I had the sobering and life-changing realization that the energy of evil was a compounded *human* force. There were specific and real human beings ultimately guilty and responsible for the terrorist act of 9/11. However, those people were affected by parents and friends who lived in a village or city affected by a culture and ideas, which was affected by the history of its civilization and geography, which was affected by the history of the peoples that surrounded it. We are all connected to the generations that precede us and the ones that follow us. Each act of cruelty or indifference affects the lives of every person and generation that follows. Our actions are cosmic, never private as we hope and think.

We live in a world that has been conditioned by millennia of human brokenness. Distorted human and social behavior is so *normal* that we accept, without argument, the universal excuse—"I'm only human"—which implies that it's inherent to our human nature to be deeply flawed. But is this true?

Gene Roddenberry, the creator of the popular television series *Star Trek*, said, "We must question the story logic of having an all-knowing, all-powerful God, who creates faulty humans, and then blames them for his own mistakes."[3] Is human nature a divine mistake, and are we hopelessly morally bankrupt? What can we expect from ourselves and others? These are fundamental questions about human identity, and in order to answer them we will look to the Scriptures—in particular, the creation story in Genesis and the Gospels of the New Testament.

The first three chapters of Genesis record the beginning of human history in the Garden of Eden. In this story we discover what can and must be recovered in our human lives. It boldly confronts us about what we see and what we don't, about the delusions we fall for and the heights from which we've fallen. Ultimately, we find hope and the path of our own redemption in this garden. If we care to be truly human, our journey must start there. So, let's return together to that holy place and retrace the steps of humanity.

## The Garden of Eden

The Garden is a place of wonder and pleasure, a place God has planted masterfully. There are no categories or distinctions between the material and spiritual worlds. It's what the Celts called a "thin place"—an intersection of heaven and earth. Each day He adorns it with different elements that make it more spectacular than the day before. It's lit by the stars in the sky and colored by the plants and trees of the earth. It's watered by springs and surrounded by the thunderous sea crashes. It's alive with activity. Plants explode with color, and vegetation produces a bounty for the innumerable insects, birds, and animals that explore it with curiosity. Everything is landscaped to court our affections and attention. We cannot stand in this place without seeing, hearing, smelling, feeling, and tasting the devotion and goodness of God. The Garden is a total-body experience of His presence and love.

Our first contact with God is in the Garden. We discover that He is mysterious and unknowable but present and personal. He lives outside of time, but every moment is filled with His presence. He has always existed, and there was never a time when He didn't love us. He needs nothing but gives endlessly. He cannot be forced to act but always shares without hesitation or limit. He has created us, and the Garden in which we meet, because He wishes to share His life. He chooses a garden because He wishes for an intimate introduction.

## Human Beings Are Created to Be Dynamic

Our creation is His finishing touch. We are the crown and focal point of God's creativity and design. When God gave form to us, everything else in the Garden made sense and found its purpose. From the soil of the Garden, He breathed His own life into us and masterfully shaped us in His image and likeness so we could share and experience His unexplainable love. We are perfectly designed to receive, contain, and share His love.

Of course, it follows that the human nature we've been given embraces the reality and trajectory of life God intended in the Garden, and it cries out like Mary in the Gospel, "Let it be to me according to your word" (Luke 1:38). Human nature is dynamically charged or magnetized toward God. We are hardwired that way. We have a natural inclination and movement toward our Maker. It is a powerful energy and orienting force that can be misdirected but never completely suppressed or erased. In its ideal state, it is rooted in the present moment and moves freely toward Him without hesitation or reasoning.

Augustine, in his book *Confessions*, is famous for writing, "God, you have made us for yourself, and our hearts are restless till they find their rest in you."

From the perspective of the Scriptures, real life means to be in communion with God, to resemble Him, to imitate Him, and to participate in His life. Those who are *truly* human will manifest the activities, or energies, of God in their lives. This is our end—to become mature in our humanity so we reflect the image of the One in whom we have been created. Spiritual growth is a natural desire for every human being.

In the middle of the afternoon, on my first day at Ground Zero, a good friend and I were assigned to work at St. Joseph's Chapel on Liberty Street, just across from The Pit. The chapel had become a makeshift relief and supply center for the countless fire fighters and law enforcement officers working around the clock.

The space was part convenience store, part drugstore, and part motel—an odd combination with the inside of a Catholic chapel. Besides the stained glass, the fixed altar was the only visible evidence that the space used to be a chapel. The commercial carpet was stained with the debris of the Pit, and the pews, candelabras, and religious statuary had all been shoved to the side or into a nearby closet. Tired men, covered in thick grayish ash, sat slumped with their backs against the walls. Our job was to help organize the supplies and make them more accessible to the workers.

After an hour or so of organizing work gloves, toiletries, and energy bars, I felt moved to shift our attention to a greater need.

I quietly motioned to my buddy, and we walked over to the altar that was lined on all sides with sleeping and duffel bags. The altar itself had been cleared off, and its usual religious hardware had been replaced with an alarm clock, an ashtray, and a variety of personal items—it had become a nightstand of sorts. Slowly and respectfully we began to remove the personal belongings. After searching the closets for altar cloths, candles, and the Gospel book, we cleaned and reassembled the altar area. The finishing touch was to move a couple of kneeler benches in front of the altar.

After lighting the altar candles, we turned around to discover a crowd of firefighters standing and kneeling in prayer. I was moved by the vulnerability and sincerity of these hardened veterans. It was a vivid example of how people instinctively hunger for something deeper than food and long for a kind of rest more lasting than sleep.

## Human Beings Are Created to Be Free

How we use the dynamic energy God has created within us is important. When we live in harmony with this divine orientation and movement, we experience genuine freedom. Freedom is not, as we sometimes believe, the power to choose—it is the experience of accepting and embracing this God-given orientation and energy that already exists in our souls.

It's similar to the natural alignment of our physical body. In order to move freely, we have to accept the natural posture and mechanics of our spine and limbs. We don't complain that our body has made us a slave to these movements, but rather accept the "efficiencies" of our natural design. If we try to move our body in unnatural ways we create constraint, awkward movements, and even pain. Through sheer willpower and determination, we can choose to move in unnatural ways, but we end up fighting ourselves and weakening our movements.

Later on, when I was serving in the family assistance shelters, I met many people who, through the events of 9/11, had become reconnected with earlier traumas in their lives. It was as though their personal experience of 9/11 had ripped the scab off even deeper wounds.

One of these people was a woman who confessed to aborting her unborn child much earlier in her life. We met several times before she was actually able to tell me the story, and when she did, it was with more human shame and agony than I have ever witnessed in my pastoral experience. As she recounted her story, her words were filled with self-loathing and desperation. And in her bitter tears was the question we all want answered: "Can God actually forgive me?" Deep in her heart, she had already answered that question, and this was the reason she was slowly distancing herself from the Church.

This woman's decision to abort her child was not an exercise of her freedom—it was a distorted exercise of her will. *Choosing* to abort her child did not bring her freedom; it brought her bondage. The irony is this: the *power* to choose a course that is unnatural to our human nature makes us weak and powerless. It is only the power to choose a natural course that brings us freedom. Unfortunately, too many of us have become enslaved to the multitude of bad choices we've made.

I told this wounded woman the truth: God forgives you, and you need to find a way to forgive yourself and reconnect with the Church. Time passed, and I left the New York City area. When we eventually reconnected, her demeanor and countenance were completely different, as though something had radically transformed inside of her.

She told me that she had been searching for her former pastor to seek his spiritual guidance. She found out that he was serving as a missionary in a very remote village somewhere in South America, but he was very sick. Undaunted, she found a way of contacting him and obtained his permission to visit him. Because of his remote location she had to meet him in the jungle, and he drove her the rest of the way to the village where he ministered. When they arrived, she wasted no time in pouring out her soul and seeking his guidance. She felt like God had spoken to her. Almost as soon as she had arrived, she turned around to return home and reunite with her Church community. In total, her trip lasted only four days. Two weeks later her former pastor and spiritual mentor died.

As I said before, I've never seen deeper grief over one's actions than I did in this woman. However, I can also say I've never seen greater resolve to find healing. By living in reality, confessing the truth about her broken life and seeking healing, she chose to exercise her will in a way that was natural to the humanity God gave her. And in the end, she found freedom from her bondage.

The experience of freedom comes to us when we recognize the connection between the material and spiritual worlds.

They are not divorced from one another. Most of the countless books, videos, and training programs that guarantee successful life management ask you to use your God-given dynamism in a way that separates the material and spiritual realities of your life. When these two realities become distinct categories with no connection, we live our lives in delusion and fail to see and hear God in everyday life.

The dynamic energy God has created within us longs to move toward Him in every moment and action of the day. He wants us to see Him at work, loving us, no matter what our reality is. There is no need to run from, hide, or rewrite the truth of our lives—in every situation and relationship, there is always a step we can take to embrace the love and truth of God. When we take this step, we experience freedom, and we move closer to Him and our own humanity.

## Human Freedom Is to Be Communal

The life of freedom God wishes for us to experience comes out of this dynamic movement toward Him and always takes place within the context of community. When God created the earth and its creatures, He said it was "good." After He created man, He said it was all "very good." The first time Scripture records God's disapproval is when He says, "*It is* not good that man should be alone" (Gen. 2:18).

God Himself, in whose image we are made, is communal—three Persons with different activities (Father, Son, and Holy Spirit) sharing one common divine nature. They eternally exist and act together in perfect harmony and love. Father, Son, and

Holy Spirit coexist in perfect humility—there is order without conflict or competition. Each of these divine Persons serves the good of the *Other*. Ultimately, the dynamic energy God has placed within us is charged by this *others orientation*. The movements most natural to our soul will always be characterized by love and will always draw us closer to God and one another.

Life is intended to be a shared experience, and it is only fulfilled in the activity of giving and receiving. Any action or reality that promotes selfishness is not *life*. In fact, as we will see in the next chapter, it is actually the experience of death. The word "idiot" in our English language ultimately comes from the Greek reflexive pronoun *idios*, which means "one's self." When we consider only our own outcome, we act idiotically and ignorantly.

Again, the analogy of the human body is helpful. Most of us have witnessed the determined efforts of individuals who have been forced to use some of their limbs to compensate for the absence or deformity of others—such as those who walk on their hands because they have no legs and feet. While we would all agree that these efforts are heroic, we would also agree that they are only made necessary because something is broken and not natural. In a human community, as in a broken body, we're sometimes forced to compensate for the brokenness of other members. Their dysfunction can affect and even harm our life.

The pain of community can even cause us to run into private worlds that distance us from discomfort and confusion. However, the reality is that these self-protected existences are only a *pseudo-life*. They do not bring the experience of freedom, but bind us up in small worlds of bitterness and resentment.

There is an interaction between these two fundamental dynamics of freedom and community. They can either be an unstoppable force of goodness in this world or the greatest source of human chaos. Depending on the exercise of our will, the interaction between these dynamics can cause either a "Cycle of Blessing" or a "Cycle of Neurotic Suffering." We will consider the first cycle here.

## The Cycle of Blessing

Our movement toward God is characterized by rhythms of awareness and response—a realization of His love for us and a reaction of thanksgiving and surrender. This rhythm or cycle is the real life God intended for us to experience, and it can be discovered in every situation and relationship—even in those where we suffer through no fault of our own.

### Awareness

In the Genesis story, God says, "See, I have given you every herb *that* yields seed which *is* on the face of all the earth, and every tree whose fruit yields seed; to you it shall be for food. Also, to every beast of the earth, to every bird of the air, and to everything that creeps on the earth, in which *there is* life, *I have given* every green herb for food" (Gen. 1:29–30). God calls Adam and Eve to *notice* His divine presence in the Garden—to *be aware* of the reality of Him in every living thing and being. We are created as sensory beings for this very reason—so that God can reveal Himself to us. When we fail to see the reality around us as a divine manifestation of His presence, we forget the ultimate reality and begin to experience distortion. We become less real.

Even when the reality of our lives or the world around us is broken, we can still see the love of God at work. We don't have to be in a remote and undisturbed setting. If we quiet our racing minds and focus in on the present moment, we can be aware of God's presence in the busiest and most chaotic contexts. When we're blind to this, we're like those who, St. Paul says, "suppress the truth in unrighteousness, because what may be known of God is manifest in them, for God has shown *it* to them . . . who exchanged the truth of God for the lie" (Rom. 1:18–25). Being aware of God's presence is the starting point for all movement toward Him.

### Thanksgiving

If we fail to see God everywhere and in everyone, we begin to forget how to respond to Him. We forget that being grateful to God is fundamental to being human. We can become like those who "although they knew God . . . did not glorify *Him* as God, nor were thankful, but became futile in their thoughts, and their foolish hearts were darkened" (Rom. 1:21). Failing to notice the presence of God leads to our own identity crisis—our minds can become confused about the real meaning and purpose of life. A thankful heart, however, is the real proof that we see God in every reality of our lives—the good and the bad.

Gratitude creates an orientation of love and trust. When we recognize and embrace that we are completely dependent upon

God for everything, we do not doubt His love or goodness. We act in ways that assume His provision in our lives. Jesus uses an example from nature to describe how normal and natural this way of life is: "Look at the birds of the air, for they neither sow nor reap nor gather into barns; yet your heavenly Father feeds them. Are you not of more value than they?" (Matt. 6:26). When we trust that we are valuable to God and that He will not abandon us, we are able to reach out to others.

### Offering

Every time we truly see and are thankful for the goodness of God in our lives, it changes us. Our natural movement toward God is strengthened, and we mature in our humanity. Thanksgiving creates a deeper awareness that we can surrender the entirety of our lives to Him. We can let go and trust His goodness. Thanksgiving naturally creates the desire to give back—to share and multiply the goodness of God. This was at the heart of God's command to Adam and Eve: "Multiply; fill the earth and subdue it" (Gen. 1:28). God wants to multiply the experience of His presence and love throughout creation, and we are intended to be His ambassadors.

In the Garden, man is the only intersection of the material and spiritual, the created and uncreated. He is uniquely gifted to unite both realities within himself. He has a vocation to notice the good gifts of God, give thanks, and surrender his life in faith. We are called to offer up the totality of our lives to God—our resources and possessions, our intellect and talent, our relationships, failures, successes—literally everything.

When we do, He blesses and transforms them into deeper experiences of His love for us.

### Communion

The result of this divine-human interaction is real communion. It completes the Cycle of Blessing and then renews it endlessly with a new and deeper awareness of His presence. This is the normal movement and rhythm of the human person—it is how we are designed. When we live in harmony with this rhythm, we experience freedom and the life God intended for us.

Any other path or success apart from this truth may feel like real life, but in fact it is not. This is the reason so many people are left feeling empty and confused no matter how much they accomplish. When we accept that we are hardwired this way, we begin to feel the real meaning and fulfillment of life. Our destiny is a shared life with God—a life that ultimately finds rest in Him, but never ceases to grow into the knowledge and experience of His infinite love.

Although we live outside the Garden today, in a world filled with hellish events, we can still orient and exercise our will in a way that moves us closer to God and brings us the experience of His life and freedom. Even in the midst of life's afflictions and sufferings, we can still reclaim a truly human rhythm to our lives that is rooted in both the material and spiritual worlds and is characterized by awareness, thanksgiving, and surrender to God.

# CHAPTER TWO

# Choosing Away Our Freedom

*After all, we're only human . . .*

—Everyone

I T TOOK SOME TIME, but eventually the American Red Cross moved into Manhattan and took over the coordination of relief efforts from the New York City Office of Emergency Management. All of the chaplains had to be rebadged and were deployed to a variety of family assistance shelters around the city. I wasn't certain how I felt about leaving Ground Zero. It felt like we were being moved off the front lines to the safety of the general's tent to push papers. I had finally become accustomed to the intensity of the Ground Zero scene and didn't know how I was going to adjust to a different pace. Little did I know!

My first shift was an early evening, at a place called Pier 94. I showed my badge at security, checked in with the Red Cross mental health supervisor, and was directed to a small room with boxes full of fluorescent-colored vests. There was no blending in for chaplains and mental health workers. I was given a short briefing and instructed to mingle among the crowds looking for opportunities to provide comfort and counsel.

Pier 94 is an enormous place, over 130,000 square feet. Normally it's a venue for trade shows, but on that night and for months thereafter it was the emotional Ground Zero for families and loved ones. When I exited onto the main floor I was shocked by the size of the crowds and the volume of temporary offices erected to serve the practical and emotional needs of the shattered families left behind. The warehouse-sized space was dwarfed by the heavy gloom of the atmosphere that night. I felt claustrophobic and could feel my chest constricting with anxiety. Almost immediately I felt disoriented, self-conscious, and insecure.

I headed toward a long makeshift wall on one side of the building papered with missing person posters, notes to loved ones, and ads for assistance—it was something between a remembrance wall and a community information board. In the moment, it felt like a place I could blend in and busy myself with something other than what I was supposed to be doing. Maybe with a little distraction I could give myself enough time to rise to my responsibilities.

I started at one end and slowly worked my way down the wall. The photocopied pictures of loved ones and desperate pleas for more information were more emotionally overwhelming for me than the destruction and chaos of Ground Zero. The Pit was a smoldering pile of twisted steel. Most victims were unrecognizable. Here, in the family assistance shelter, the faces of death and grief were inescapable. Tears were streaming down my face as I moved from one photocopied memorial to the next.

I was about two thirds down the wall when my eyes were drawn to a brightly colored picture. It was obviously drawn by a young child. I leaned close to see the young artist's signature. It was the work of a little girl, age nine. The drawing was a picture of two different worlds, like what you would see from outer space. Above and below the picture there were separate captions with arrows pointing to each globe. One of the worlds looked like earth, complete with oceans and what looked like the continents of North and South America. The arrow led back to a caption that simply stated: "This is my world with my Mommy in it." The other globe was colored completely black and footnoted by a caption that read: "And this is my world without my Mommy in it."

At that moment I felt grief like I had never experienced in my entire life. I thought of my own young daughters. How could something so awful be placed on the shoulders of someone so young? I simply couldn't imagine the fear and pain inside this little girl's heart. Her world would never be the same.

My head was pounding, and my face ached from the repeated attempts to hold back the tears. This was a level of emotional darkness and desperation that I had never faced in my pastoral vocation. I was only twenty minutes into my first shift, and all I could think about was getting out. I stumbled away from the wall in a daze. I wandered among the crowds, traumatized and desperate to escape.

It must have been written all over my face, because a fellow chaplain stopped me and asked how I was doing. I choked back my tears and tried to regain my composure. But I knew he could see the fear in my eyes. He comforted me by sharing his own first experience with the wall, and slowly he talked me down off the ledge. I finished my shift that night, but when I went home and crawled into bed, with my two little girls fast asleep in the next room, I was forced to make an adult admission: this broken world leaves all of us victims.

Carl Jung, the well-known Swiss psychologist, said, "There is no coming to consciousness without pain."[4] Events like 9/11 force us to reflect on *why* questions, like "Why is there evil?" And, if a good God exists, "Why does He allow it?" If we are made in the image of an intelligent God, these are fair and reasonable questions, and the same Scripture that informs these questions also gives us the answers.

We know from the first three chapters of Genesis that God created only what was good. It's the human distortion of this good that we call evil. God allows this distortion, because to prevent it would require Him to restrict our free will, and without free will, love and relationships are impossible. By definition, love assumes the possibility of rejection. There is no such thing as love without risk. This is why the Genesis account records not only the creation of mankind, but also the rejection of God.

## The Two Trees in the Garden

At the center of the Garden of Eden, God plants two trees: the Tree of Life and the Tree of the Knowledge of Good and Evil. Eating from the Tree of Life is encouraged and considered normal; however, eating from the other is strictly prohibited. God warns Adam and Eve that they will die if they eat its fruits—clearly an experience God does not desire for His creation.

The test of Adam and Eve's freedom comes in the form of a serpent, whispering questions of doubt: "Has God indeed said, 'You shall not eat of every tree of the garden'?" (Gen. 3:1). The question subtly *interrupted* man's natural trust in God. The serpent suggests with his question that God has withheld something good from their experience.

Eve is forced to hesitate and recall God's instructions. When she replies, she affirms God's permission to eat from all the garden fruit except from the tree at the center, but then adds to the command by saying that they are not allowed to *touch* the fruit. Already, the serpent's seed of doubt has begun to sprout. Eve's perception of God has made a slight shift. The serpent's question suggests a negative interpretation of God's command, and now Eve's focus has shifted from the wonder of God's abundant provision to the possibility that there is something lacking or missing in her personal experience.

This slight shift opens the door for the serpent's next challenge: "You will not surely die [if you eat or touch the fruit]. For God knows that in the day you eat of it your eyes will be opened, and you will be like God, knowing good and evil" (Gen. 3:4–5). In other words, *real life* can be found in something other than God, and He is intentionally trying to hide it from you through rules and commands. Perhaps Eve begins to wonder whether or not God really wants to share His life or if His intentions can be trusted at all.

Modern marketing uses the same technique: There is

something missing in your life that you presently do not have, and you are therefore incomplete in some way. You need product "X" to make your life or experience complete. Marketing executives exploit what is most basic to our human nature, our desire to be made whole. Every human being has a natural drive toward completion and maturity; we find it unbearable to know we are lacking. When this drive finds God as the target, we experience freedom. However, when it runs in other directions, we experience endless distractions, frustrations, and suffering.

The serpent promises Eve that she can shortcut her dependence upon God and create her own reality. He even guarantees she will be "like God, knowing good and evil" (Gen. 3:5). The serpent's unspoken message is now clear: You can find real life apart from God, and, in fact, you can become your own god, knowing what is best for you and others. Furthermore, it can be found right here and right now in the garden.

For the first time, Eve deliberates. She's hesitant and conflicted about the meaning of the fruit—is it a sign of God's goodness and provision, or evidence that He is the great killjoy in the sky? Up to this moment, it was natural for her to trust in God's goodness, but now the seeds of doubt have infiltrated her mind and distorted her thinking. It is from this unnatural context that Eve exercises her will to eat the fruit from the forbidden tree and then convinces her husband to do the same. "[They] exchanged the truth of God for the lie, and worshiped and served the creature rather than the creator" (Rom. 1:25).

Immediately Eve discovers it is true what the serpent has

promised: "your eyes will be opened." Unfortunately, what she and Adam see is not what they expected. They find enlightenment, but not the kind the serpent promised. The Bible says, "the eyes of both of them were opened, and they knew that they *were* naked" (Gen. 3:7). Their shame and subsequent hiding from God in the Garden is evidence that they are no longer moving toward God, but are falling away from their natural human vocation. Instead of finding freedom, they find shame and fear—so much shame and fear that they run and hide from God. Then come the blame and the excuses. Adam: "The woman whom You gave *to be* with me, she gave me of the tree" (Gen. 3:12). Eve: "The serpent deceived me" (Gen. 3:13). And so begins the fallen trajectory of man that leads to its dysfunctional but logical conclusion: "Cain rose up against Abel his brother and killed him" (Gen. 4:8).

The word most often used for "sin" in the Bible is the Greek word *hamartia*, which literally translated means to "miss the mark." With this understanding, the picture becomes clearer. Adam and Eve, whose target and end was to become like God, missed the mark of their goal and fell away from God and their calling. They exchanged the truth about God for a lie and exercised their will to *choose* a path different from what came most natural to them. They chose to forge an existence independent of God. The result was cosmic. When they *chose* this path they found slavery instead of freedom, and death instead of life.

This fallen trajectory of mankind creates another kind of cycle very different from the one we discovered in the previous chapter. It's a cycle built on lies. The foundational lie that Adam and Eve believed was that there was a life apart from God, a life they could create on their own. They failed to understand that life will always include God, because He is the Giver of Life.

When the eyes of Adam and Eve were opened to their actions, they experienced what God never intended: death. Death is more than the cessation of a human heartbeat. It is the reorientation of our human vision and activities away from the life of God. There are infinite variations of this broken and distorted human experience, but it always has the same end—the fragmentation and delusion of the human person.

## The Cycle of Neurotic Suffering

The Bible records the tragic consequences of this fundamental shift in human orientation. In Genesis we read "Adam . . . begot a *son* in his own likeness, after his image, and named him Seth" (Gen. 5:3). While Adam and Eve were created in the image and likeness of God, their children and future generations were born in the broken physical, mental, emotional, and spiritual image of their parents. While every human person, because of their common human nature, bears the indelible stamp of God's image, the descendants of Adam inherited that image in a radically distorted version. We have inherited a cycle of suffering and slavery from our parents, and they from theirs.

When we reflect on the common and predictable activity of broken humanity, we see it can be summarized into a vicious cycle of three stages: *victimization*, *survival*, and *perpetration*.

### Victimization

The initial truth of this cycle is hard for some of us to swallow: we are all born into a broken world, and eventually we are *victimized* by it. Most of us would never use the word "victim" to describe ourselves, but in fact each of us experiences, to some degree, the common realities of abuse, loss, and abandonment. Each of these comes on a sliding scale and is very personal and subjective.

You might be a person who downplays these kinds of realities. You're slow to point the finger at anyone except yourself. You take responsibility for your actions and believe that no one else should be blamed for the quality of your life. In general, this is a good perspective from which to operate—as long as it does not lead us to suppress a greater truth about the reality of our lives. The world in which we live is broken and filled with broken people. The evidence is all around us. Every day we are affected by the reality of this context. Yes, we are responsible for managing those effects, but we are and have been affected. Sometimes we have been affected more deeply than we care to admit, especially in our childhoods. These are the realities we must face with honest reflection.

We're not born guilty for our parent's sin, but eventually their broken lives, and the lives of others around us, affect us in ways that lead to our own fragmentation. Each of us was created to be loved perfectly and completely, but no matter how sincerely our parents try, our experience of love is always incomplete. They can never love us with all of the love we were intended to receive, the love of God. This is the reality of life outside the Garden.

If you ask my children they will tell you I make one request, over and over again. I tell them someday they will come to the realization that their father didn't love them perfectly, and that epiphany may come with painful memories and emotions. When that happens, I've begged two things of them: first of all, give me the chance to make it right by coming to me with those honest memories and feelings, and let me ask forgiveness face to face; secondly, let me help pay for the therapy bill.

### Survival

All this results at best in a frustrating experience, and at worst in a painful existence. In this worldly context, we struggle in order to cope and survive. We don't get the love we deserve and need, and so, from a very young age, we instinctively try to make our reality as comfortable as possible. Over the course of a lifetime, we manufacture a whole series of pseudo-selves and scripts that give us a sense of identity, meaning, love, and control, and help us live with others and ourselves.

After I finished giving a talk at a retreat on this very topic, a young lady approached me to talk about forgiving a family member who had repeatedly taken advantage of her sexually. To make matters worse, her mother and father were aware of the abuse but failed to stop it. They encouraged their daughter to overlook it in order to keep the family peace. Eventually the advances came to an end, but this young lady was left deeply wounded. As the tears streamed down her face, I didn't need to ask her how she had coped with the pain over the years—it was obvious.

I looked at her and said, "People have told you how beautiful you are your whole life, haven't they?" She nodded in the affirmative. For most girls, that kind of attention brings security, albeit a security that can lead to its own brokenness. For this young lady, however, it brought the feeling of terror. In her mind, beauty was connected with abuse—so she ate.

"You're afraid, aren't you?" I asked.

"Afraid of what?"

"You're afraid that if you lose weight men will be attracted to you and you'll run the risk of abuse all over again," I answered gently. She nodded again as she sobbed uncontrollably.

We all want to avoid the discomforts of life—whether they're physical or relational. When we can't, we feel out of control and desperate. We seek to control people and situations so we can manage our thoughts and feelings about our world and ourselves. But sometimes the thoughts and feelings become so unbearable that we are driven to escape into activities that damage us even further—things like addictions and co-dependent relationships.

Most of us regularly manufacture and manage what we believe to be an *acceptable* reality. To be truthful, however, it's a delusional reality. We create private worlds where we can suppress our thoughts, numb our feelings, and relate to people in fictional ways. This gives us a false sense of well-being and control over our lives—it makes them bearable. However, the more we live this way, the more fragmented we become as human beings—we continue to *fall away* from our true end.

### Perpetration

The problem with these delusional activities is that they only work temporarily, and they usually leave us feeling even more anxious and desperate. When one type of control doesn't work, we work harder or become creative and try different variations and kinds. Eventually, our anxieties create angry and desperate emotions that are usually expressed in our most intimate relationships. We complete the Cycle of Neurotic Suffering by victimizing others through our broken lives. Sadly, the ones we often victimize are the ones we love the most.

The beautiful young lady I counseled who had eaten in order to cope with the trauma of her sexual abuse eventually developed a romantic relationship with a young man struggling to figure out his feelings of homosexual attraction. She wanted to know what it felt like for someone to love her for who she was, and he wanted to know what it felt like to love someone without guilt. It was safe for her; it was safe for him. What they didn't realize was that they were unintentionally using each other to cope with the pain in their own lives.

It's not comfortable to admit we're victims or that at times we're just surviving, but nobody wants to confess that they've hurt someone else, especially someone they love. The truth is, however, all of us unintentionally harm one another in our attempts to protect ourselves. It's easy to be so focused on guarding our own identities and egos that we roll over others in the process. No amount of good motives and intentions can erase the emotional, and sometimes physical, damage we can do when we're trying to control others or a situation for our own benefit.

Parenting is an obvious example. As I've already said, we're all victims of imperfect parenting. Most of us have had parents with unquestionable motives and intentions, but we still came out with scars. Despite our parents' deep love for us, they were trying to survive their own pains and suffering. As a result, sometimes we were the emotional victims of their coping mechanisms. They, like us, didn't set out to harm anyone else, but the reality is that they did, and we do too. When we can face up to the reality that we often victimize others in an attempt to manage our own pain, we reach a spiritual turning point.

This Cycle of Neurotic Suffering and delusion can quite literally be an experience of hell on earth. We find ourselves helplessly losing control over the things and relationships in our lives that are most important. We feel out of balance and incomplete, tired and worn out, unhappy and unfulfilled. The harder we try, the more we hurt, and the more we hurt others. We're left to believe that the only solution is to escape and start over. In most cases, however, the problem is usually not our situation, it's us. Until we can honestly accept the broken reality of our lives and desire our true humanity and natural movement toward God, our lives will remain in this downward spiral.

Ultimately, the goal is not to remove suffering from our lives, but to transform it into a redemptive experience. Like Christ on the Cross, we can abandon ourselves to the will of God and offer up our suffering in anticipation of His mercy. In these moments, we become truly human.

# CHAPTER THREE

# The Logic of Suffering

*The concept of Hell is "I am my own."*

—George MacDonald[5]

D URING MY DAUGHTER HANNAH's junior year in high
school she formed a friendship that troubled her. Her
friend was subsisting on food stamps and wore the same clothes
day after day. Her friend lived with her dad and older sister not
far from us. The father was out of work and both sisters had
jobs at competing fast food restaurants near their home. Both
sisters were very bright, but they struggled to maintain good
grades because they worked so much. There were regular stories
of unpaid bills and a less than ambitious but demanding father.
As troubling as all of these details were, I sensed that there was
a deeper issue here, and I wanted to understand what it was.

One day after school, Hannah asked if I could give the friend
and her sister a ride home. I agreed, and they directed me to an
extended-stay hotel. For Hannah's friend, her father, and her
older sister, home was one room with two queen-sized beds, a
sink, and a stove. They had been living that way for over a year.

The sisters dreamed of going to college, but I wondered if it was possible without their father's support.

Despite their daily challenges, the girls seemed to function without self-pity or any real evidence of depression or negativity. Hannah always described them as happy and positive. The girls got out of the car that afternoon without the least appearance of embarrassment and politely thanked me for the ride. As we left the parking lot, I empathized with Hannah. Her friend was living a broken existence, far from her own control.

One night during the spring semester, Hannah snuggled up next to me in her usual way that let me know she wanted to talk. Her friend, her older sister, and her father had just collected their income tax returns. Between the three of them, the IRS returned over five thousand dollars. It was a windfall for this struggling family and the chance to gain some financial traction and stability. My mood brightened as she told me the story, but then I saw my daughter's facial expressions fall.

She told me that after paying a couple of small bills, the father took the money to the casino and lost everything. Apparently, this was a well-established pattern—one that left the girls working and wondering whether or not they would have enough money for food and rent. What a life, I thought to myself. The girls must feel completely vulnerable and out of control. But, I imagine their father feels the same way.

## Psycho-Logic

Hannah's story illustrates the cycle of suffering described in the previous chapter: victimization, survival, and perpetration.

While it's easy to judge the actions of this father as irresponsible, self-consumed, and unloving, there is a "psycho-logic" to his behavior. He may even justify his actions as an effort to care for his family. The crisis of gambling away the family's money is symptomatic of deeper issues.

The dysfunctional logic that fuels the cycle of suffering is the subject of this chapter. Whether it's gambling, substance abuse, self-mutilation, or any other variety of high-risk behavior, it seems completely crazy and illogical to most of us why certain people would want to inflict trauma upon themselves over and over again. It's easy to judge someone else's actions as self-defeating and destructive, but most people engage in these behaviors for a reason.

The fact is, everyone suffers from an identity crisis—it's our broken inheritance from Adam and Eve. Eventually the pain of these broken identities and the situations they create becomes so immediate and intolerable that a person feels compelled to act in a way that most of us would consider illogical or pathological. The fact is, all of us instinctively avoid pain, sometimes even when we know our method of avoidance will cause more and greater suffering downstream.

Every person has a different threshold and set of resources to meet the personal challenges they face. Our personal makeup is complex and as unique as our own thumbprint. There is so much we inherit, physically, mentally, emotionally, and situationally, over which we have no control. We have no choice but to play the hand we've been dealt. Many times the challenges seem to outweigh the resources we have, and we make poor decisions that lead to real crisis—for us and for the ones we love. From an outsider's perspective, these decisions and actions may seem stupid and senseless, but to the person who is desperately running from an unbearable burden they seem to be the most logical path. There is a *logic* to every dysfunctional behavior.

There are essentially four components to this psycho-logic: *beliefs, perceptions, feelings,* and *actions.* Each component builds consecutively on the component preceding it. Suffering begins with a *belief system*—about life, people, relationships, success, etc. Our belief system develops over a lifetime, formed largely by our parents' belief system and our own experiences. Most of the time, we're unaware of this life orientation, but it's the cornerstone of all our judgments. It reveals what each of us believes to be true and false, real and unreal.

From these building blocks of *personal truth,* we form *perceptions* or interpretations about our experiences. Correctly defining and understanding perception is key, because it is never truly objective. There can be ten eyewitnesses to a bank robbery and ten very different accounts. Each person brings a variety of personal and experiential lenses to a situation. The result is always a *subjective* interpretation—thus the saying, "Perception is reality."

The personal experience of suffering begins when we perceive that our reality is unbearable and out of control. Our perceptions give way to *feelings.* Generally, when we feel out of control it triggers a self-protective and aggressive emotional response—fear, frustration, anger, bitterness, resentment, etc.

These feelings can be directed outward or inward, but they are always characterized by a deep dissatisfaction with the way things are.

These emotions become the fuel and motivation for our subsequent behavior, which is the final component of suffering. The *actions* that evolve out of our psychological need to gain control or equilibrium are always some kind of compromise—that is, they are not the direct actions we wish we could take. Solving the problem directly is either out of our control or doesn't feel personally safe. Therefore, we take other indirect actions, often fueled by fight-or-flight emotions. These can come in a variety of forms, including passive-aggressive behaviors and addictions.

Hannah's friend's father believed he could create his own reality. At the very least, he was willing to take the risk of creating his own reality. Perhaps this risk came from a place of real pain—the pain of not being able to adequately care for the practical needs of his daughters. Perhaps he felt completely out of control and unable to steer the dictating circumstances of his life. If so, it's not *illogical* to think he would be willing to engage in high-risk behaviors. The real crisis here is not the gambling, but the unbearable personal pain. It is this pain that ultimately fuels the delusional belief that he can control his reality through gambling.

Once his mind is convinced that he can change his reality through high-risk behavior, everything and everyone is filtered through this delusional lens. He interprets people, including his own daughters, and situations as either allies or enemies of his plan. He must, because the only other alternative is despair and defeat, and those are the very things from which he's running. At this stage his mind is made up, and there is very little anyone can do to change the course of events. He cannot see any other options. An associated or random crisis of greater pain is the only possible intervention at this point.

With a plan firmly in place, he already feels a sense of control and relief. There is a false sense of hope and happiness that comes over him—a lightness he has longed to feel. These delusional beliefs fuel the fantasy of what his life, and his daughters', will be like once he feels in control again. The more he rehearses this fantasy, the more resolved he becomes to take action, and the more convinced he becomes that it is the logical and right action to take.

By the time he engages in the risk, he has tunnel vision. So when the weight of the risk and its consequences begin to be felt, he commits himself fully and dives even deeper into the behavior. He believes that if he turns back at this point, not only is there no hope for personal control over the pain in his life, but there will also be nothing left of his personal self-respect or identity. He's convinced that his acceptance from others depends completely on his ability to be in perfect control of his life. He believes it's do or die.

The tragic and cyclical reality is that as this father *awakens* from the delusion of his actions, the associated feelings of pain and regret will only deepen his desperation for control. Desperation is the mother of vicious invention. These risky behaviors will most likely continue, and his daughters will be further victimized. Unfortunately, his daughters are the victims. They, too, are experiencing the feelings and consequences of being out of control and the associated personal pain. Soon, if it hasn't already happened, they will find their own unhealthy ways of coping with and surviving this reality. This is how the cycle of suffering is handed down from one generation to the next.

This is a common thread through every human story, beginning with Adam and Eve—the fracture begins in the mind. Our mind is the pilot of our bodies and souls. It's designed to be inspired and moved by God's Spirit, which directs us naturally and freely toward God. When our minds are tempted and governed by other sources, such as our bodies and affections, our course is misdirected and we become lost in a sea of competing thoughts and confusion. Our minds become clouded, and we make poor decisions that lead to suffering and separate us from our communion with God, ourselves, and others.

The phrase "train of thought" is applicable here. If we are still long enough, we can observe that thoughts race through our heads like speeding trains, endlessly strung together by free association and/or logic, and impact with real force the way we think, feel, and act. What happens in our heads has real consequences in our lives. It is the battlefield on which the spiritual life is won or lost.

## The Vices

Christian saints have long recognized the importance of this battlefield and identified certain patterns of thoughts that lead to suffering. These thought processes have been categorized into what we commonly call the *vices*. There are a number of lists throughout history, including those in the Scriptures. Perhaps the most well known is the Seven Deadly Sins popularized by Dante, the poet, in *The Divine Comedy*. Some of the lists contain seven vices, some eight, and some even more.

The vices that cause the greatest suffering are *gluttony, lust, greed, anger, self-pity, despair, vanity,* and *pride*. These vices can be broken into three categories: (1) physical—gluttony, lust, and greed; (2) emotional—anger, self-pity, and despair; and (3) spiritual—vanity and pride. Each of these vices and categories has a psycho-logical connection to the rest.

Vices begin in the mind as a string of connected thoughts and reasonings based on our beliefs and perceptions. Eventually they lead to distorted behaviors that demonstrate an improper use of our human will and freedom. At their root, all vices share a clouded vision of reality, a delusional outlook on life. The experience and living out of these vices is the story of humanity. By understanding the psycho-logics and interconnectedness of these vices, we will begin to see the areas of our own life in need of healing and develop a deeper empathy and compassion for others who struggle with them.

### Gluttony

Food is a primary connection and means of communion with God. It's a daily sign that God cares and provides for us. For this reason, when we eat it is to be accompanied with thanksgiving.

Gluttony, however, is a distorted relationship with food. It deceptively promises that we can find fulfillment, and not just sustenance, in food. Food is such a fundamental part of our lives that we can be tempted into believing that we exist to eat, and not eat to exist. For many, food allows an escape into an alternate reality. Eating is an easy activity in which they can engage and be in control. The pleasure and control of food can dominate in such a way that food becomes a replacement for real living.

## Lust

Relationships are also a primary connection and means of communion with God. In another person, we can recognize the image of God and experience His love. The experience of community gives us the necessary context to experience life as God intended. In order for community to work, though, each person must take the other seriously and respectfully. It requires that each of us recognize the image of God in the other and act accordingly.

Lust is a relational distortion—a self-centered orientation toward the other. It asks the questions: What can I get? How can I be satisfied? How can I use the other to please myself? It sees other people as objects or body parts, not as human beings made in the image of God. The pleasure of lustful behavior, which can manifest itself in thought or action, can create an addictive and delusional world of control, pseudo-connectedness, and personal significance.

## Greed

Greed is systemic to both gluttony and lust, because food and relationships are treated as possessions and not gifts. Gifts are from God's goodness and are meant to be shared. These gifts and pleasures remain good as long as they are used as a means of communion with God.

Greed, however, is the distortion of this human stewardship. It reduces a human person to a selfish consumer and hoarder. Consciously or unconsciously, greed leads us to believe that God has *not* given us everything we need for real life; therefore, we take things into our own hands. Ultimately, greed leads to idolatry because it makes possessions, not God, the focus of goodness and life.

Gluttony, lust, and greed are *gateway vices.* They are a distorted attempt at creating another reality—one that feels acceptable to us. The question is: What happens when these vices don't work, or leave us without the emotional fulfillment we expected?

Typically, we dive in even deeper, hoping for different results. The reality is, though, that vices never solve our psychological and emotional needs; instead they lead us even deeper into a vicious cycle. One vice leads to another, usually more destructive and harder to uproot than the previous one. When the possessions of gluttony, lust, and greed fail to give us the experience of real life we were all created to desire, we usually experience one or a combination of three other vices: anger, self-pity, and despair.

### Anger

There is an anger that is pleasing to God, a just anger that is motivated out of love for God and/or others. But most often, anger is our initial reaction when things don't go *our* way. It's an immature and misdirected kind of human zeal. Instead of being moved by a godly justice, we are moved by a kind of self-centered justice where we appoint ourselves judge and jury. Our judgments lead to impatience, spite, revenge, rage, and hatred. Once the emotions of anger are ignited, they are difficult to extinguish. Whether it is directed outward or inward, anger is always a poison to others and to ourselves.

## Self-Pity

Not to be confused with real grief, the vice of self-pity is a kind of depression that colors all of life and results from a self-centered orientation. When the delusional reality we seek to create and control doesn't satisfy or work out, it's often accompanied by immature emotions of grief, fueled by anger turned inward. This inward-facing anger can lead to pouting, silence, passive-aggressive behavior, complaining, gossip, tantrums, whining, etc. This kind of selfish sadness can paralyze us. For this reason, ancient Christian writers often use *sloth* interchangeably for this vice.

## Despair

When anger and self-pity go unchecked, they ultimately lead to despair. It is the end result of our failure to live in reality. Despair distorts our vision so that we can only see absurdity and futility. Life loses meaning and seems hopeless. We become indifferent to situations and people and begin to dig ourselves into deep pits of self-absorption. Like those suffering from self-pity, we begin to experience a lack of energy and motivation. We feel useless and lose our desire to pray—largely because we no longer experience hope in God. For this reason, despair is the most dangerous of all the vices. When despair takes hold, we begin to believe that we are outside of God's grace and power. The isolation and the hopelessness are an experience of hell on earth.

The experiences of despair and futility lead a person to question his identity, self-worth, and significance. In the Garden, man's identity is informed and secured by God's goodness and love. But outside of the Garden, there is only confusion, and man is at a loss to understand his true calling and direction in life. As a result, over the course of a lifetime, he tries on different identities, looking for something that brings him a sense of security, acceptance, and significance.

### Vanity

Vanity is man's attempt to piece together an identity apart from God. It's not so much a singular action or vice as much as a web of vices seeking to capture and control self-significance and happiness. It's a complex collage of human activity evidenced by misguided forms of attention seeking. You see this on Facebook all the time—people who constantly update their profile status and photo, seeking admiration for their opinions, achievements, and latest look.

Social media's insidious allure comes from the false promise that we can manufacture our own identities. It's impossible for us to self-create our own identities—they are given to us by God. We are created for Him, and it is only in Him that our human nature is fulfilled.

## Pride

Pride is both the beginning and end of all the vices. In the Garden, Adam and Eve were captured by the seductive suggestion that they could become "like God." They fell away from their love of God into self-love. When their selfish actions turned into shame, their vision became clouded by the crisis of their broken identity. This provided the opportunity for every other vice to take root. Pride believes that we are the center of our own realities and that our human efforts can forge a meaningful life without God. It assumes that we know what is best for ourselves, and often for others as well. It goes hand in hand with vanity and cyclically feeds all of the other vices. For this reason, it's called the mother of all vices. Pride is defensive, argumentative, stubborn, self-directing, shortsighted, and slow to listen. It is easily masked by pseudo-spirituality and is the most difficult vice to uproot.

The psycho-logic of neurotic suffering is engrained even deeper into our societies by the advent of modern media. All of the *vicious* thinking patterns have been given a new power through the new modes and avenues of digital communication. The allure of virtual lives and identities is endlessly paraded before us. We now have high-definition temptations to shortcut our experience of real life. In reality, however, it's an old lie with new promises.

The only way to experience the freedom of real life, the divine life God created us to enjoy, is to reorient and realign our humanity as God intended it. Our minds have hijacked and taken hostage our entire human identities. Despite all of our efforts to control our own reality, the fact is, we are controlled by the thoughts that barrage our minds. Most of us are unconsciously fixated on either the past or the future. The present moment is an uncomfortable experience for us, and rarely do we know what to do with it. We are constantly anxious about what has happened or what could happen. This kind of life not only affects us, but everyone else around us. Most importantly, it separates us from God and His divine life, which are only available to us in the present moment. If we wish to recover our humanity, we must get out of our heads!

# CHAPTER FOUR

# Waking Up

*All truths are easy to understand once they are discovered; the point is to discover them.*

—Galileo[6]

O N MY SECOND VISIT TO JERUSALEM, I explored the city without a guide or tour bus. I wanted to experience the city myself and without someone else's commentary and political or religious bias. I walked the endless cobblestone streets of the Old Market, explored the various quarters of the Old City, visited some of the holy sites, and ate at local restaurants off the beaten path. One morning, I exited the Christian Quarter of the Old City through the New Gate. I saw a sign for the Church of St. Peter, and I took the bait.

As I hiked down a long road, the King's Valley was to my left. My mind wandered to the City of David as I spied the steep slopes and countless rooftops of the valley. I wondered about that moment when King David, while walking on the rooftops of his palace, looked on Bathsheba as she bathed, and the course of Israel was changed forever. As the scenes from this biblical narrative flashed through my mind, an unusual sight in the distance suddenly caught my attention. Jutting out of the steep hillside was a golden rooster perched upon a black cross and centered on a blue, tiled, Byzantine domed roof. "How odd," I thought to myself. It's not uncommon to see a dove paired with a Christian cross, but I'd never seen a farm animal atop a church roof. Was this the Church of St. Peter to which the sign was pointing? I picked up my pace.

Soon I approached a parking lot and saw signage for the Church of St. Peter in Gallicantu (Latin for "cock's crow"). Immediately I felt a sense of anticipation and hurried to the front entrance below the parking lot. The main church was an impressive Byzantine structure in the classical shape of a cross. This particular church building was erected in 1931, but I later discovered that the first chapel on this site dated back to AD 457. The front entrance was adjacent to a courtyard filled with a four-figure metal statue scene from Luke 22. The inscription read: "But he denied Him, saying, 'Woman, I do not know Him'" (Luke 22:57). The scene was sobering and strangely haunting; I couldn't help but think that there was something providential about my visit.

As I entered the front doors, an explosion of color fell from the stained glass cross stretching over the expanse of the domed ceiling, painted in deep blue and covered with stars. The Church was busy with visiting tour groups. I found a chair and sat quietly in the back of the nave. I felt as though I were sitting under the heavens. Despite the bustle of people, the space was peaceful and reflective. After a while, I noticed a group exiting downstairs. I decided to follow and queued up behind them as we filed down a long staircase.

The staircase opened into another chapel carved into the hillside. Massive stone walls from the hillside protruded into the chapel, and there was a glass railing encircling a large hole in the middle of the nave peering down into an ancient cave with crosses carved into the stone walls. The chapel was remarkably simple. There was an altar, three Byzantine paintings, and some chairs. The group filed out relatively quickly, and I was left with just a few others. I sauntered to the front of the chapel and sat down in the first row of chairs.

I was immediately transfixed by the three paintings. I was familiar with Byzantine art (also known as iconography) and its normal religious themes, but there was something strikingly different about the works in front of me. The icons on the left and the right were outside the altar area and smaller than the central icon located directly behind the altar. They were a set—like a triptych without hinges. They read left to right, like a book, and told the story of Peter's denial with an emotional depth I had never seen or experienced before.

The icon on the left depicted Peter's denial of Christ in the courtyard outside the high priest's residence. Peter and Christ are the central figures with the accusing servant and guards in the background. Jesus and Peter stand facing each other, eyes locked in the stare of an eternal moment. It was the moment that "the Lord turned and looked at Peter. Then Peter remembered the word of the Lord, how He had said to him, 'Before the rooster crows, you will deny Me three times'" (Luke 22:61).

It must have been a moment much like the one when Adam and Eve realized they were naked. It's that gut-wrenching moment when the curtain of our delusion is lifted and we realize that nothing is hidden to God. I felt Peter's desperation as I looked at his broken ego and pride, spilled in colors all over the icon. The colors were rich and bright, but the mood was dark and speechless. What is there to say when you have denied Christ?

Between 1949 and 1952, the Communist Party in Romania carried out what has become known as the "Pitesti Experiment." It was designed to "reeducate" political prisoners through sadistic stages of unimaginable psychological and physical torture. The prisoners were subjected to regular and escalating experiences of intense confinement, humiliation, physical labor, interrogation, brainwashing, and beatings. The final stage was their forced participation in the "reeducation" of new prisoners. Many of the prisoners literally went crazy and/or killed themselves as a result.

One of the inmates in the Pitesti prison was Fr. George Calciu. Fr. George wrote about his experiences in a book entitled *Christ is Calling You!* In it Fr. George confesses his repeated denials of Christ, under torture, and the unspeakable emotional pain that ensued. He writes:

> It was a spiritual fight, between good spirits and evil spirits. And we failed on the field of battle; we failed, many of us, because it was beyond our ability to resist.... When you were tortured, after one or two hours of suffering, the pain would not be so strong. But after denying God and knowing yourself to be a blasphemer—that was the pain that lasted.... We

forgive the torturers. But it is very difficult to forgive ourselves. You knew very well that the next day you would again say something against God.

And knowing that he would deny Christ yet again, Fr. George admitted that it was "in the night, when you started to cry and to pray to God to forgive you and help you, [this] was very good."[7]

It was this kind of bitter pain and tearful repentance that was the subject of the next icon, directly behind the altar. This icon was the largest of the three and, as in a traditional triptych, intended to be the centerpiece. It was an icon I had never seen before or since. It pictured Peter sitting on a rock, with his head hung low and cradled by his hand. There was a hollow expression of disbelief on his face, and in the background a dark ominous cave engulfing his painted figure. While painted tears were not visible from my distance, the scene was clear. The words of Scripture echoed in my ears: "So Peter went out and wept bitterly" (Luke 22:62).

Tears streamed down my face as I sat motionless, stunned by the profound and personal significance of this image. "There I am!" I thought to myself. "I know the despair of that dark cave and the bitter sting of those tears. I know that empty, incredulous look." The icon screamed, "What have I done, and what will I do now? Will He ever forgive me?" I felt it pulling me further and further under until my gaze wandered to the last icon.

In the final icon, Jesus and Peter are depicted on the familiar seashore of Galilee with a campfire surrounded by bread and fish in the background. Jesus is extending a shepherd's staff to

Peter. It is that post-resurrectional narrative where Jesus asks Peter, "Simon, *son* of Jonah, do you love me?" (John 21:16–17). After repeated attempts, Peter answers, "Lord, you know all things; You know that I love you" (John 21:17). Yes, Jesus does know everything. He knows that our love is weak and faithless. But despite this, He extends to us the staff of our vocation. He calls us back in love to that path for which we've been created.

From the evening campfire of despair to the morning campfire of hope, these three icons moved me through the emotional and theological reality of repentance. The colors and figures displayed without words the movement of spiritual reorientation. I felt exhausted and renewed all at the same time. Most of all, I felt a deep and overwhelming conviction of Christ's abiding love.

Peter is emblematic of each of us. We can see our own lives in each of these icons, and it is our repentance that the Lord wants. He wishes for each of us to come face to face with the brokenness in our lives and admit to the distorted persons we've become. Each of us has a real history of self-love and treason against God. We have denied God in our actions, words, and thoughts. The connecting piece between this realization and our reorientation is reflection.

Real reflection requires us to live in reality. So often, we rehearse the past with fresh and delusional interpretations that justify our role and actions. But repentance is difficult. It asks us, to the best of our ability, to look at ourselves in the present moment as we really are and ask, "What have I done, and who have I become?" It requires the courage to stand nose to nose with our actions and the humility to own them. For many of us, it's unbearable to think on these things. Our egos are already too frail and damaged to admit to more failure. But Christ doesn't wish to drown us in our failures. He wishes to restore us to our true identities—identities made to experience the depths of His love. As long as we hold onto who we are not, we will never be able to recover who we were always meant to be.

Our human vocation, outside the Garden, is to continually reorient our lives. We have fallen away from what is most natural to us, and we must therefore reorient our bodies, minds, and souls toward God. The Greek word used in the New Testament for "repentance" literally means to "change one's mind." In order to restore our humanity, we must change the way we think and orient ourselves toward life.

## Personal Inventory

This kind of reorientation requires a thoughtful inventory of our lives and some awareness of what areas have become distorted. The discovery of these places can take many forms, both formal and informal. Furthermore, this is not something that happens just once. Humans are dynamic beings, always changing and growing. Realizing the truth of one's self and reorienting is an ongoing process throughout life. We experience more truth about our reality and ourselves the more we step into the light we already have.

Embracing this reality begins with asking the right questions. In order to understand the unique logic of our personal distortion and suffering, we need to ask ourselves the uncomfortable questions concerning our actions, feelings, perceptions, and beliefs. In many cases, you will want to ask those closest to you for their observations. Our distortions always reveal themselves in the contexts most familiar and intimate to us—marriage, family, work, church, and friendships.

Some of the questions we will need to ask ourselves will concern our childhood and family of origin. At this point, many people just want to move on. They ask, "Why should I waste my time reliving painful events and relationships? What's past is past. I need proven strategies to move forward with my life." There is truth and delusion in those comments. Reliving the pain of our lives without purpose is a waste of time, but reflecting on one's history in the presence of a trusted friend or spiritual advisor with the goal of growth is never a waste. Those who ignore their history of suffering through compartmentalization or repression are certain to repeat it.

Asking questions about the historical suffering in our life, especially early childhood pains, can lead to significant personal discovery. As we discussed earlier, all of us experience some kind of victimization in life, and for many of us that happens most significantly early in life when we are most vulnerable. Physical, mental, and emotional suffering experienced in childhood forces us to develop creative, and sometimes relatively sophisticated, coping mechanisms. Children are more emotionally intelligent and resourceful then we give them credit for. The need to be loved and accepted is a powerful motivating force. Unfortunately, the mechanisms we develop as children to secure acceptance affect our beliefs, perceptions, feelings, and actions. And without intentional reflection, we can become stuck as adults with the emotional skill set of a child. This becomes problematic in all of our relationships, especially with those with whom we are most intimate.

## Identity Paths

There are five basic questions we can begin using immediately to build a personal inventory. I call them *identity paths*. These questions act like paths that lead us back to what we really believe about ourselves—the truth and the lies. When used in conjunction with the psycho-logic model, explained in chapter three, they can help us embrace the distortions of our lives and who we've become. They can be used once or with regular frequency, but they should always be used with the help of someone else. The Scriptures affirm, "The heart *is* deceitful above all *things*" (Jer. 17:9). We should always be untrusting of self-judgment and the actions it suggests to us. It's best to ask the help of a discerning therapist, pastor, family member, or friend. Ultimately, they can help us better understand the ongoing resources we will need for the healing of our humanity.

The key with each of these questions is to process them in the presence of someone you trust to tell you the truth in love. Be careful to make observations without judgment or interpretation. Hold the analysis, verdict, and application until the very end of the process. Here's how it can work for you: (1) In the presence of your confidant, ask yourself one of the five questions and note whether your answer centers on a behavior, feeling, or perception; (2) use the psycho-logic model in *reverse order* (behavior > feelings > perceptions > beliefs) to ask a series of questions concerning the previous components in the psycho-logic cycle.

For example, if your answer to one of the questions centers on a *behavior*, then you would ask yourself a follow-up question concerning the *feelings* behind your behavior—"What was I feeling when I did that?" From there you would ask yourself a question directed at the *perceptions* behind those feelings—"What kind of filters or interpretations did I have that led to those kind of feelings?" And finally, you would ask yourself a question directed at the core *belief* behind those perceptions—"Why did I interpret my situation that way, or what is it that I really believe about that situation?"

This reverse psycho-logic process helps us to make honest observations about the sometimes automatic and unconscious reactions that make up our efforts to cope with painful situations and create equilibrium in our lives. Once we have arrived at the core beliefs behind our behavior, we should ask the person with whom we have shared our thoughts to share their observations and insights. Are our personal beliefs built on distortions of the truth? Identifying the lies that dictate our broken behavior is the cornerstone to the healing of our humanity.

In the fourth chapter of Matthew, Jesus meets in the wilderness the same serpent Adam and Eve encountered in the Garden. The devil tempts Jesus by quoting Scripture three different times, and Jesus counters each temptation also quoting the Scriptures. As we noted in the second chapter, every temptation has at its root a lie. With perfect discernment, Jesus is able to preserve the natural movement and integrity of His humanity by living in harmony with the truth of Scripture. Answering the following questions will help us determine the lies we have come to believe and the truths we must relearn by faith. Remember, it's not our behavior that is the crisis. Our actions are only symptomatic of the real crisis, which is what we believe.

**Question #1: What are the painful circumstances, relationships, or habits in my life?** It makes good sense to begin with the most obvious and sensitive issues in our lives. When we chip away at the cornerstones of our suffering, we make progress in so many other areas. Suffering and vice are like a well-connected web that stretches over the course of our lives. When we pull down one of the corners, the rest of the web begins to collapse as well. What are the historical sore thumbs of our lives? What are the pains from our childhood? Are there significant relationships we have lost or in which we have felt unacceptable, unloved, or abandoned? Are there addictions or persistent habits in our lives over which we feel guilt or shame?

**Question #2: What are my fears and anxieties?** We all experience worries, doubts, and panic about a variety of reoccurring subjects. These kinds of emotions provide us with significant evidence that our psychological orientation has become abnormally fixated in certain areas. Why do we perceive these particular areas in our life as threatening? What do we really believe is the worst-case scenario? Are we trying to gain authority or power over people or situations outside the immediate scope of our responsibility and control? Do our anxieties paint a black-and-white version of the world? Do our fears take into account the love and mercy of God?

**Question #3: What are the tapes that regularly play in my head?** Scientific research has revealed that our brains think four times faster than we speak. This means our distorted minds are narrating messages at the speed of six hundred words per minute—that's over a half million words in a typical sixteen-hour day. Most of the time, we're completely unaware of the scripts that are playing out in the background of our minds. The question is: What kinds of messages and beliefs are our minds reinforcing? Are they true? What do they reveal about our perceptions? Do they naturally direct us toward faith in God and love for Him and our neighbor?

**Question #4: What do others say or perceive about me?** This can be a helpful or risky question, depending upon whom we listen to. If the comments come from someone we respect and trust, we should listen carefully. The book of Proverbs says, "The law of the wise *is* a fountain of life" (Prov. 13:14). But if we suspect that a person's comments are selfish or ill-motivated, we should weigh them with discernment. Thinking through the recurring comments we have heard about our personality and character over a lifetime will be the sole means of confirming or challenging what we are discovering in our answers to the other questions.

**Question #5: What do my daily actions, attitudes, and conversations reveal?** Because the immature coping mechanisms of our childhood usually follow us into our adult lives, our natural daily reactions, attitudes, and replies can be very revealing. Reflect on an uncomfortable situation or interaction you've had within the last twenty-four hours. How did you respond? What did you feel? What were your perceptions? Which beliefs do the answers to these questions reveal?

Creating an inventory of painful experiences from our past can be an emotionally overwhelming task. Most never make it past the initial consideration. The mountain seems too large and too steep. The good news, however, is that there are many beneficial resources to walk us through the process. I've used a combination of other resources in addition to the identity paths above.

At a variety of times throughout my life I've seen a personal therapist, and I expect it will happen in the future. Finding the right therapist is very personal. Therapy is built on trust, which is a very subjective reality. Sometimes it requires visiting more than one therapist before you find the right fit. There were times, however, that I couldn't afford the hourly rates of a trained professional. This forced me to research good materials written by trained professionals. One resource I found particularly helpful was *Changing Course* by Claudia Black. Her book provided me with a very simple and methodical process to work through the experiences of my past. To this day, I still review the notes and journal entries from that process.

In addition to these, don't overlook the power of pastoral and community-based resources. I'll never forget the moment this entire process began for me. During an intimate conversation with my seminary dean, he asked me very pointedly, "Kevin, where does the anger inside of you come from?"

Shocked by his question, I incredulously replied, "I don't know."

He fired back quickly, "If you don't figure that out and get a handle on it, you'll be confessing it the rest of your life."

He was right. The next week I took his advice and began to attend a local twelve-step program that opened up a world of healing in my life. Neither of these resources cost me a dime. I've learned over time that all truth is God's truth. There is no hierarchy or separation of truth into categories—spiritual and secular. If something is true, it comes from God—regardless of its context.

Many years later, as my seminary dean edited a copy of this manuscript, he wrote in the margins that he wished he would've worded his counsel differently. He wrote: "We *can't* 'figure it out.' We have to be purified and illumined to *see* where it comes from—through a multi-faceted therapeutic process that takes time, effort, courage, patience, and lots of help from others. Psychological counseling [or group therapy] *must* be accompanied by spiritual counseling, which need not be with a pastor… [It can be with a] trusted, loving, and non-judgmental brother or sister in Christ, and in a process that literally never ends."

Now I take most of my new insights learned from therapy, community programs, or reading and discuss them with my pastor or spiritual mentor. This provides me with another level of depth and perspective in my journey toward maturity. It helps me to integrate my emotional and spiritual lives. And often, it helps me understand the next step I should take. The resources that are right for you depend largely upon your time, finances, and personality. Regardless of what resource combination you use, there are two things you should keep in mind.

First of all, make sure the resources you use are credible. Credibility has many sources: academic and professional training, personal and peer review, and, of course, professional experience. Make certain that you are entrusting your emotional well-being to a trustworthy source. Ultimately, you want resources that assist you in finding the truth about yourself and your experiences. Half-baked counsel can lead to risky emotional and relational consequences.

It's not mandatory to use resources that have PhD training and/or experience, but it is imperative that you entrust the most vulnerable experiences of your life to discerning people and resources. Finding these is an intuitive and providential process. Pray about it. God will lead you in His love.

Secondly, make sure the resources you use provide you a safe context to be completely honest about your past and present life. In order to make real progress, we must have emotionally safe contexts where we can admit what we really do, think, and say when people are around and when they're not. This kind of trust doesn't happen overnight, but when we're finally able to reveal the secrets and distortions of our lives, the healing and maturation process takes place exponentially more quickly. The revelation and application of truth in a safe context is powerful and life-changing medicine.

The self-knowledge gained from these resources will begin to paint the real picture of the pseudo-self you've constructed over the course of your life. They will reveal the story of your victimization as well as your perpetration. If you can accept and own these painful realities, you will have exercised the courage and humility necessary to take the first step in your journey toward becoming truly human. One of the ancient Christian writers said, "It is a greater miracle than raising the dead for a person to see himself as he really is."[8] But once we see ourselves and our need for healing, we can run to the Great Physician and the hospital in which He practices—the subject of our next chapter.

# CHAPTER FIVE

# Becoming Human

*Now with God's help I shall become myself.*

—Søren Kierkegaard[9]

I'VE ALWAYS BEEN a hopelessly visual person. I need maps, diagrams, pictures, and, yes—instructions. It's difficult for me to grasp certain concepts without some kind of pictorial representation. The spiritual life is no different. It's memorable and particularly helpful to me when I can see Christian virtue acted out in someone I know. That's the reason why, in 1994, I made my first trip to a monastery. I was intrigued by the stories about a simple priest who served the nuns at a convent in south-central Michigan, enough to make the eleven-hour drive from Memphis, Tennessee. Fr. Roman Braga, like Fr. George Calciu, was a survivor of the Pitesti prison in Romania.

I first met Fr. Roman on a cold, sunny day. He was wearing a heavy coat and hat. His body was slightly bent, and he clutched a cane for balance. When he entered the refectory with the abbess of the monastery, he greeted us with an angelic smile. When he removed his monastic cap, his bald head revealed a large scar on one side of his scalp. His conversation with us was short and simple, but I remember being struck with his almost childlike demeanor.

Over the course of the weekend, I had several more encounters with Fr. Roman, mostly in a group setting, after church services. He spoke freely to us about his imprisonment, without revealing details of his torture or suffering. And he expressed his gratitude for the experience that gave him Christ. He spent his first year in solitary confinement. He lost his sense of time, and of seasons. "In that situation," he said, "the only place to go was inside. There I discovered an inner universe—God and myself."

Later in an interview he said, "They [The communists] couldn't control what is inside of you . . . [It] was good because there in prison we were praying . . . you are placed in a cell, there is nothing else . . . Not having anywhere to go or even look out a window . . . you have to look, to go somewhere; and so you go inside yourself, inside your heart and inside your mind to examine yourself, to see who you are and why God brought you into this world . . . You find God when you know yourself . . . [You] have to remain in Christ and to accept Christ by saying: 'Lord, come, I am here. You created me. Open my heart because You created this heart. You created the door, enter please.'"[10]

On the last night of my stay, Fr. Roman graciously granted my request to speak with him in private. Most of the details from our conversation that night are a blur to me. What I do remember, however, was the way I felt. To this day, I have never experienced such an overwhelming feeling of unconditional love from any human being. He had a tangible and radiant joy that appeared so natural to him. His compassion for me, and my personal story, was simple and unpretentious—a kind of love that felt so very present and accessible. There were moments when I felt like he saw straight through me, but without judgment. I left our time together with a feeling of lightness and freedom.

The next morning as I drove away from the monastery, I couldn't stop thinking about him. For the first time in my life, what it meant to be human seemed strangely tangible to me, and it had never been more attractive. I went to the monastery expecting to see the miraculous and left having touched someone deeply human. What did that mean? Even though I had a theological degree and had heard a lifetime of sermons, I needed a living sermon. Through impossible suffering and a lifetime of spiritual struggle, Fr. Roman reflected the life of the only person in history ever to be truly human—Jesus. It was Jesus whom I had encountered over the weekend.

Many of us mistakenly assume, consciously or unconsciously, that Jesus is completely dissimilar to us. We think that Jesus can't intimately relate to our humanity because He was God. Perhaps some of us even think that Jesus used His divinity to *cheat* in His human experience—that's why He was able to resist temptation and forgive His enemies when hanging upon the Cross. The truth is that it's difficult to imagine someone who is truly human, because everyone we know has failed. The Scriptures teach, however, that Christ was fully human in every way.

In the person of Christ we can find the power to recover our broken and lost humanity, and people like Fr. Roman are living witnesses to this reality. Though humanity has steered a course far from its intended destination, and the consequences have been cosmic, God never abandoned His love for us. From the beginning He was the initiator in our relationship—He revealed Himself to us. And when we fell away from Him, He did not stop pursuing us. Throughout history He sent us His law and His prophets, and when humanity neglected and ignored these, He sent us His own Son, Jesus.

Christians talk a lot about salvation, but why do we need saving, and how does it work? The Bible says that the consequence of our falling away from God is death—physical and spiritual. Through the exercise of our own wills, we enslaved ourselves and became hostages to death—a condition God never intended for us to experience. This condition left us powerless to actualize the true purpose of our human existence, which is to be united with God. But God, in His love, could not bear to see His children held captive, so He sent His Son, Jesus, to pay the ransom for our freedom.

## God's Obedient Son

The human species is a dying species, subject to death like every other plant and animal on this planet. This death, however, is unnatural to us, because we were made to be far more. We were made for the immortal life of God. When we turned from God, we brought death on ourselves. It was not an act of divine vengeance or anger. God has nothing to give us but Himself.

If we will not have Him—His life—we die. Man crafted his own death. The Incarnation is that point when God chose to do what our species could not do for itself. He chose, through His Son, to place divine life back into our dying species. The Son of God Himself entered humanity with all that He is as God, recreating our nature.

When Christ entered our world, and even more so our flesh, he did not insulate Himself from its frailties. Instead, His life was subjected to poverty, hunger, temptation, and all that the human race had brought on itself. Unlike us, though, Christ endured it with love and obedience to the Father. And over the course of His life, He refashioned our species from within, reuniting our nature to God.

As children created by and dependent on God, all of us owe the Father our obedience and love. These are the most natural movements of our human nature. We have distorted these, however, into a self-centered kind of allegiance and love, neglecting our human vocation. Instead of seeing God as the only source and sustainer of life, humanity has been duped into believing life can be found in other places and things.

In the Gospels, however, we witness the man Jesus perfectly obeying and loving His heavenly Father. He knows the truth and obeys it. He doesn't hesitate in the face of temptation, because He is completely clear about His mission. His whole life is an offering of thanksgiving to God. In His famous Sermon on the Mount, He tells His disciples He has come to accomplish the writings of the Law and the Prophets—to do what every human before Him has failed to do. Jesus' offering to the Father was His life—a perfect life of love and obedience.

The life He lived was full of truth and light. It perfectly revealed His Father's identity. The religious leaders of His day felt threatened, however, and they crucified Him. And in His death, He became the perfect offering of human love and obedience to God. When He died, the human debt was paid—everything was made right.

While the Crucifixion is often spoken of in Western circles as a sacrifice that reconciles humanity to God (and this is certainly true), a deeper nuance is often ignored. In the Gospel of John, Jesus references His future glory not in terms of His Resurrection, but in terms of His martyrdom. The prologue of John's Gospel mirrors the creation account in Genesis; however, unlike Genesis, in which man's formation is incomplete (i.e., the likeness of God is never attained), in the Gospel of John, we hear Pilot utter the words to a beaten and bloodied Jesus, "Behold the Man!" (John 19:5).

In Jesus' martyrdom, we see man cling to God in the face of every adversity, brutality, and temptation. As Paul says, He was "obedient to *the point of* death" (Phil. 2:8). The scandal of this should not be missed. The Old Testament Law states that anyone hung on a tree is cursed by God. Jesus' obedience to the Father is so absolute that it includes even this public and cursed act. And in this act, as He prays for His enemies, we hear the ultimate exclamation of human history: "It is finished" (John 19:30).

Finally, here in the martyred Jesus, we find the making of man is complete. He has conquered every passion and manifested every virtue, clinging to the immortal life of God. In the dying Christ, we see for the first time someone truly human in both image and likeness. He does all of this not for Himself but on behalf of humanity. He does what we could not through our broken obedience, contrition, and good works. We were bound by death. But the Son of God, by entering our species, was able to offer up a journey back to God that culminated in the defeat of death and the remaking of humanity into what we were meant to be from the beginning.

Jesus was insistent throughout His ministry that no one would take His life from Him. Even on the Cross, His death was voluntary. And when He entered into death like every other human being, He did so with one difference—He was sinless. Death had no rightful claim over His life. When He willfully gave Himself over to physical death on a cross out of love for His Father and for us, He entered through the gates of death as a human being, bringing Paradise with Him and declaring to all of humanity its liberation from the tyranny of death. And so His Father raised Him from the dead.

Death enters with Adam and his descendants, but eternal life enters with Jesus. He is the second, final, and *real* Adam who demonstrates what it means to be truly human. It is not possible for death to hold Jesus, because death is the result of separation from God, and Jesus is in perfect communion with His Father. His very presence in the grave crushes death's authority over humanity, and the grave bursts open as it is filled with His life. It is here that Jesus declares His victory. These truths are captured so beautifully in the fourth-century Paschal Homily of St. John Chrysostom:

Let no one fear death, for the Savior's death has set us free.
He that was held prisoner of it has annihilated it.
By descending into Hades, He made Hades captive.
He embittered it when it tasted of His flesh.

And Isaiah, foretelling this, did cry:
Hades, said he, was embittered, when it encountered Thee in
    the lower regions.
Hades was in an uproar because it was done away with.
It was embittered, for it was abolished.
It was embittered, for it was mocked.
It was embittered, for it was slain.
It was embittered, for it was overthrown.
It was embittered, for it was fettered in chains.

It took a body, and met God face to face.
It took earth, and encountered Heaven.
It took that which was seen, and fell upon the unseen.

O Death, where is your sting?
O Hades, where is thy victory?

Christ is risen, and you are overthrown!
Christ is risen, and the demons are fallen!
Christ is risen, and the angels rejoice!
Christ is risen, and life reigns!

Christ is risen, and not one dead remains in the grave!
For Christ, being risen from the dead, is become the first fruits
    of those who have fallen asleep.

To Him be glory and dominion unto ages of ages. Amen!

All of this He accomplished in love for every human being, past, present, and future—whether they want it or not. In one of the ancient Christian paintings of the Resurrection, Christ is depicted standing victoriously upon the shattered gates of death, pulling Adam and Eve out of the grave with Him. The painted detail of this activity is purposefully theological. Christ is shown grabbing hold of their limp and powerless wrists. Knowing they are unable to save themselves, they desperately and desiringly stretch out their other hand to the only One who can rescue them from their deceptive captor. It is a touching and moving detail, full of theological insight and application. It captures the two necessities for the salvation and recovery of our true humanity: Christ's power and our desire.

I've often heard Christians ask the question, "Are you saved?" The Apostle John says that Christ "is the propitiation for our sins, and not for ours only but also for the whole world" (1 John 2:2). If this is true, then the answer for *every* person is a resounding "Yes! I am saved by the loving sacrifice of Jesus on the Cross." His victory over death is universal—everyone is saved by His loving sacrifice. This is the Gospel—God's Gospel in His Son Jesus. The *real* questions is: "Do we want to be saved, and to have a new life?" The former question addresses the power of Christ to save; the latter addresses our awareness of His power and our desire to be saved.

When we look at the detail of this Resurrection painting, it calls out to us individually: "Christ has made death a portal to new life. Do *you* want to be saved?" Answering this question is our only point of participation in salvation—do I want the love of God or not? And as we ponder the answer to that question, the stories of so many biblical characters surface, not the least of whom is Mary. In the New Testament Gospel according to

Luke, the Archangel Gabriel comes to Mary with a hopeful but frightening message: "You will conceive in your womb and bring forth a Son . . . He will be great, and will be called the Son of the Highest" (Luke 1:31–32).

The Scriptures say that Mary was troubled. You can only imagine the anxieties racing through the mind of this young and God-fearing teenage girl. The personal and social consequences for an unwed pregnancy in Israel were severe. But despite the whirlwind of uncertainties, she replies with courage and singular conviction: "Behold the maidservant of the Lord! Let it be to me according to your word" (Luke 1:38). And in this timeless moment, Mary reverses the double-mindedness and disobedience of Eve. She says "yes" to God, and as a result, Jesus, the true Adam and Savior of the world is born.

Salvation is both cosmic and relational. Jesus victoriously conquered death by His sinless death on the Cross, but every person must decide whether or not they want this freedom and love. I genuinely believe most people don't actively say "no" to Christ. I do believe, however, most people are actively or passively hypnotized by their own needs and desires—good and bad. Their lives and minds are too busy to reflect on the "one thing needful" for their life.

Our motivation, or lack thereof, to reach out for Christ's saving hand stems from our own self-awareness and understanding. Our souls can scream out to God even through the pain in our lives, but if we fail to live in reality, we won't make the connection. Do we see ourselves as broken and enslaved, or do we believe that we are already free?

This is a very difficult distinction to make in the modern world, where most of us live in free societies. Americans like me proudly proclaim that we live in a free nation. We have a brief history, but it's filled with the stories of heroes and martyrs who have championed our way of life. Most have family members and friends who have even risked their lives for American freedoms. But as we already learned in chapter two, genuine freedom does not come from preserving a smorgasbord of choices or rights—it's the byproduct of living a life in alignment with our God-given identity and destiny.

Fr. Roman understood faith and freedom deeply because of his contrasting experiences. He said of his life before prison, "Our faith was superficial because you can learn a lot of things and can have a mind like an Encyclopedia . . . [but] even if you know everything in the world you are superficial if you do not ask yourself who am I? Why do I exist? What is the destiny of my life? Why did God create me? If I believe in God, what does God want from me? These things when you live in freedom you do not ask yourself because you are in a hurry to do a lot of things . . . you do not have the time to meditate on who you are."[11]

It was in solitary confinement that Fr. Roman came to realize there were two different kinds of freedom—exterior and interior. He alludes to this distinction in another interview given to PBS's *Frontline*, where he said, "the human spirit is an explorer," but we neglect it by focusing on our "existence outside of ourselves."[12] Interior awareness and exploration are not widely encouraged by modern society. It's the awareness of our exterior needs and desires that is rewarded.

Exterior freedom is defined by the right to choose, but ultimately it is powerless to save. It gives human beings the illusion of control, but, in fact, it is only enslavement to ignorance and selfishness. Adam and Eve were expelled from the Garden because they saw creation as an inalienable human right to possess. Instead of witnessing the love and goodness of God in every aspect of creation, they could only see their own selfish appetites.

Because of their willful rebellion, God gave them exactly what they desired—the experience of life independent of His communion—life *outside* the Garden. The independent life man desired was no longer characterized by beauty, life, and abundance, but struggle, sweat, mortality, and murder. The freedom he desired from God's commands left him enslaved to the dictates of his merciless passions.

The freedom Christ offers releases us to become who we were created to be and fills us with real power to live and experience the mystery and wonder of life. If we desire this kind of freedom, we must let go of all our attempts to save ourselves and entrust our lives to the Creator and Lover of our souls. Letting go is not easy, though. Over the course of a lifetime, we've tied our identities and egos to a myriad of anchors. Cutting ties with these anchor points can be scary and may trigger withdrawals. The preservation of ego is a driving motivating force for most human beings. Placing faith in a new identity is difficult, and it requires a lifetime of daily decisions—saying "yes" every day to new anchor points.

This is the reason why Paul in the New Testament refers

to salvation as not only a singular event, but also an ongoing process. He says in his letter to the Corinthian church that "the message of the cross is foolishness to those who are perishing, but to us who are *being saved* it is the power of God" (1 Cor. 1:18, emphasis added). The "message of the cross" is a message of death to one's false self. Being a Christian requires letting go of these false identities and daily uniting ourselves to the resurrected life and humanity of Christ. This new identity is achieved through our desire and the saving power of His life-giving Spirit, within the community of the Church.

## A Return to the Garden

In the final book of the New Testament, the Apostle John reveals the Church being readmitted to the Garden of Paradise. Through Adam's self-love and disobedience all of us inherit a broken experience of life, but through the perfect love and obedience of the Second Adam, Christ, the gates of Paradise are reopened. This means all of us have the potential to experience life as God intended.

If we are ready to suffer with Him and willing to take up our crosses to be co-crucified with Him, we don't have to wait to taste the life-giving fruits of this heavenly Paradise. Every day provides us an opportunity to reenter the garden of life through the indwelling of Christ's Spirit. We can take notice of every good gift and sign of God's love around us, giving thanks and surrendering ourselves to His will. In the same way that our daily lives can be a hellish experience, they can also be a foretaste of the heavenly Kingdom to come.

We don't need a different life; we need new eyes to witness those things to which we were previously blinded. We can see life through the lens of our false self and its broken appetites, or we can see it through our resurrected humanity and its desire to be connected to God. We can say "no" to the worldly wisdom of the serpent and "yes" to every step that moves us closer to the communion of God's presence and love. We can experience the freedom and joy of living in harmony with our God-given nature. In these natural activities we can relearn what it means to be truly human.

# CHAPTER SIX

# Checking Yourself In

*The Church is a hospital for sinners, not a museum for saints.*
—Timothy Keller[13]

O N APRIL 15, 2013, two homemade bombs exploded near the finish line of the Boston Marathon. Three people died, 180 were injured, thirteen lost a limb or a portion of a limb, and nearly a dozen more are struggling to keep theirs. One of those amputees was thirty-eight-year-old Heather Abbott of Rhode Island. She and her best friend, Jason, were visiting a nearby bar when the blasts went off. The second blast blew Heather through the restaurant doorway, leaving her left leg severely injured. While everyone scrambled to the rear exit, she struggled to move, crying out for help.

Eventually, Heather made it to Brigham and Women's Hospital, where she underwent two different surgeries to clean and stabilize her leg injuries. The hospital introduced her to several different amputees, all of whom were athletes. Each had successfully transitioned back into normal life and encouraged her to do the same. Heather decided to undergo a third surgery that took her left leg just a few inches below her knee.

Heather is just beginning her long road to recovery. Now that the surgeons have reconstructed what they can of her leg, she will face months of daily physical therapy, phantom pains, and post-traumatic stress. Her success in recovery will depend completely on her ability to embrace new habits. She will be seeing professionals from a variety of different fields, medical and psychological, and each of these will have different therapeutic prescriptions for her to follow. She'll not only be learning how to walk again, she'll be learning how to live again.

Success in the spiritual life is similar. Every Christian is learning how to walk again and how to live again. Each of us has lived a life of multiple identities and is struggling to find our true human identity. The long-term, therapeutic success of our healing is dependent on relearning the fundamental movements of our human nature.

Like the human body, our souls have a God-given structure and design for movement. When we, by the grace of God, observe the natural mechanics of this design, we experience the freedom (or virtues) and progress of normal spiritual movement. When we choose to live contrary to our design, we experience the mental and emotional bondage (or vices) of our distorted movements. Our bodies were designed to push, pull, rotate, extend, and flex; our souls were designed to orient, commune, worship, obey, sacrifice, and witness. With time, these repetitive movements lead to normal spiritual development and maturity.

When there's an injury to the human body that disables

movement, most people elect to undergo all the necessary procedures, including surgery, hospitalization, and extensive physical therapy, to regain their personal freedoms. The Church exists to provide this same healing and rehabilitation for our disabled souls. The only obstacle is our own blindness. When a physical injury prevents us from moving, it is readily apparent to us. However, when there's spiritual injury to our souls we often miss it, because the false self we're operating with doesn't live in reality. We don't recognize our spiritual sickness because the pseudo-identity we've assumed is delusional about what's normal and what's distorted.

Furthermore, this false self is constantly in self-preservation mode. It's intolerable for us to be socially unacceptable, so we rationalize and justify our vices in order to create a sense of personal equilibrium. In other words, we're willing to embrace whatever brings us the experience of peace or internal relief, even if it's temporary, anesthetic, and delusional by nature.

Sooner or later the pain and suffering of these vices lead to personal crisis—it's an inevitable law of the created universe. These relational and situational crises are only symptomatic though—the real crisis is the disability of our souls. Despite the destructive effect these crises have in our lives, each unique situation provides us with a potential turning point to reorient and choose healing. Pain has a unique way of stripping away all of the methods we use to protect our pseudo identities. With enough suffering, we are usually left feeling vulnerable and open to change. These are the moments when we're most aware of our spiritual sickness and when we are most willing to give our consent to the spiritual medicine of the Church.

The Church is God's redemptive gift to broken humanity. It is a community set apart to bring healing. This comes by way of the Cross through Jesus, the Great Physician, who died on it and rose again to new life. Every person who checks into this spiritual hospital is recreated through the death and Resurrection of Jesus Christ. This is the reason why baptism is the central symbol and sacrament of reorientation in the Church. It is the normal and visible consent for treatment.

## Orientation

Baptism is important because it so clearly identifies each patient with the first fundamental movement of the human soul—*orientation*. Through baptism and the descent of the Holy Spirit in the form of a dove, Jesus identified Himself with and was anointed for His Father's mission. His purpose and orientation were always clear. Jesus assumed everything it means to be human so that He could reveal to us everything it means to be divine. All of His words and actions were loving and truthful, and as a result He is the "light of the world" (John 8:12; 9:5). Through His love and obedience to the Father, He perfectly revealed what it means to fulfill the human mission.

All of us have a predetermined mission in life. We are called to "be partakers of the divine nature" (2 Peter 1:4) as He partook of our human nature. Growing into the likeness of God is the most natural and intuitive dynamic of our souls. It literally defines our humanity. The problem is that we have buried this dynamic with the vices of our false selves. We have practiced the vices of our life with so much repetition and conviction that this intuitive movement toward God no longer feels natural to us.

Shortly before my fortieth birthday, I decided to take on a very aggressive exercise routine. The program involved lots of bodyweight exercises like pull-ups and push-ups. Each month I did hundreds of each. But after only six months, I developed a serious repetitive stress injury in my right elbow—most often called "tennis elbow." It was very painful. On most days I had difficulty raising my arm past a certain point without an intense burning sensation. My doctor sent me to a physical therapist, with whom I went through weekly therapy for months.

Each week the therapist would isolate the affected muscles and tendons by prescribing very specific exercises, which we would rehearse together so I could do them at home by myself. What surprised me was how simple the prescriptive exercises were—so simple there was a real temptation not to do them at all. I forced myself to do them every day, even though sometimes I felt a little silly doing them. With time, my tendonitis resolved, as the therapist promised.

The Church has offered certain prescriptive exercises throughout its two thousand years of therapeutic practice. These transformational habits help us to recover the functional movements of our humanity. In the case of our lost orientation, the habits of repentance, confession, and spiritual direction are key.

Repentance is subject to personal awareness. Every Christian should seek to know him- or herself as plainly as possible. This means understanding, to the best of our ability, the truth and effects of our past and present. Denial and repression are the enemies of the human soul. These two coping mechanisms lay the foundation for most of our false identities. In order to be truly human we must admit to the reality of the pain and emotion that comes with our personal history. We must also admit to all of the ways in which we tried to cope with the pain and anxiety of our histories. This means confessing to what we really said, did, and thought—when people were watching, and when they weren't.

The Scriptures teach us to confess our sins to God, but they also say, "confess *your* trespasses to one another" (James 5:16). We must practice both, making certain we are not hiding from the truth. It is a willful act of defiance against the false self to confess the brokenness of one's own life to another human being. Our vices breed in the darkness of our secrets. Speaking the truth concerning our words, deeds, and thoughts crushes the stronghold of our vices and strengthens the freedom of our true identity in Christ.

Each of us needs to find a safe person and be completely truthful with them about the reality of our lives. This shouldn't happen just once, but with regularity throughout every season in our life. The more often we confess, the more we strengthen the identity and orientation of our true self. The person with whom we share does not have to be educated in theology or therapy; in fact, the benefit of our confession is in no way dependent upon the person who hears it. Ideally, though, the person to whom we confess is a mature person who can listen without judgment and accept us unconditionally.

We should also seek out a person who could, if asked, offer

some discerning and honest direction for our life. It is not enough to confess; we must also be willing to submit ourselves to the maturity and experience of others. Self-determination is a gift God gives to each of us for the purpose of orienting ourselves toward Him; self-direction, however, is a delusional byproduct of our own self-protective pride. Each of us should seek the wisdom and truthful counsel of others who can, with discernment, help us orient our lives toward the Kingdom of God.

## Communion

The right orientation will always lead us into *communion* with God and our neighbor. Orientation is the course heading, but communion is the destination. We were created as communal beings—to love and be loved. Despite the risk and pain of love, we cannot be truly human without embracing it. This is nowhere more evident than in the life of Jesus, who joyfully accepted His Father's mission of love. Throughout His ministry He revealed the risks and sacrifices of communion with His fellow man. What a mystery to reflect on, how the Lord willingly subjected Himself to the free will of the beings He Himself created. What humility! The Cross is the evidence of Jesus' great love and steadfast orientation. Through His own death and Resurrection, Jesus reveals the path to communion with God and one another.

This functional movement of communion can only be restored and strengthened through habitual selflessness. This does not mean accepting abuse from others or the practicing of self-abuse; rather, it is an admonition to our selfish hearts.

Sacrificial acts crucify our vices. We must commit to them whether we feel like it or not.

Each of us has multiple contexts of community: our marriages, families, friendships, Church, and work. Each of these gives us the opportunity to "pay forward" the grace, mercy, and unconditional love extended to us. We must be careful of becoming like the unmerciful servant in Scripture who demanded instant payment from his debtor (Matt. 18:23–34). The natural movement of communion in our lives can only take root if we do for others what has been done for us, most especially the mercy and forgiveness of the Cross.

The personal awareness that leads to our repentance and reorientation should also make us aware of the struggles of the people with whom we interact everyday. All of us fight a great battle in this life, and all of us long to be accepted and loved. It's for this reason that we act so irrationally. The habitual practice of selfless behaviors like patience, forgiveness, long-suffering, kindness, and gentleness are the only weapons powerful enough to conquer the demeaning actions and words of others. Jesus' Passion on the Cross is evidence of this. Above all, we must strive to always be cognizant of God's image in every human being. Every person, regardless of how dark his or her behavior may be, is worthy of our honor in some fashion. Each person is worthy of honor because each bears the image of God. There are no casual interactions—they are all divine encounters.

Our heavenly destination is not only communion with God, but also with all the faithful who have gone before us. The Scriptures describe the experience of heaven as a communion or gathering around the throne of God. All of us come together in perfect harmony and orientation. The mansions, golden streets, and pearly gates are metaphors to describe the city of our common dwelling and brotherhood. We must begin practicing in this life for what we hope to attain in the next.

## Worship

The communion of the heavenly life is not ultimately something for which we have to wait. The Church calls us to this gathering and experience each Sunday in memorial of the Lord's Passion, death, and Resurrection. We gather together as a resurrected community and orient ourselves in *worship* around the throne of God. According to the Scriptures, we step into an eternal experience outside of time. We join our voices to "an innumerable company of angels . . . [and] to the spirits of just men made perfect" (Hebrews 12:22–23). Together we worship, listen, give thanks, surrender, commune, and are sent out into the world as the light and fragrance of Christ's love. We offer our bodies as living sacrifices to God, in and with Christ. In this movement of worship, our souls are nurtured and healed, and our human vocation is fulfilled.

Everything within the walls of the Church is centered on Christ, and there should be no distractions to this focus. The worship, teaching, sacraments, and fellowship of the Church reveal Christ and make Him present. The services of the Church answer the question Jesus posed to His disciples: "Who do you say that I am?" (Luke 9:20). Through communal worship, Christ's identity and ours are revealed. In this experience we meet Him as He really is and as we really are.

There is no substitute for this experience. It cannot be replicated on the golf course, in the woods, or out on the water. While communion with God can be experienced in all these places, they are not the Church. Communion and community are not something the Church has or gives; it is what the Church is. Only as the Church do we gather as the resurrected Body of Christ and worship Him in "spirit and truth" (John 4:23–24) with the angels and the faithful who have gone before us; only as the Church do we experience a clear vision of the entire cosmos and the role God has appointed for us in it; and only as the Church do we receive the grace of healing that comes from communal worship, teaching, fellowship, and participation in the sacraments. These are the medicines that reform and heal.

## Obedience

In the movement of worship we hear the public reading and explanation of the Scriptures, and we are reminded that, like Jesus, our heavenly Father has given each of us a mission. This mission is only fulfilled through *obedience*. Jesus demonstrated His submission to the Father and took "the form of a bondservant, *and* coming in the likeness of men . . . He humbled Himself and became obedient to *the point of* death, even the death of the cross" (Phil. 2:7–8). And even in the grave, He "committed *Himself* to [God] who judges righteously" (1 Pet. 2:23). Jesus did all these things out of obedience to the Father whom He loves. He came to do His Father's will "on earth as *it is* in heaven" (Matt. 6:10).

Our human mission is not something we make up or figure out through personal inventory tests; it is revealed to us in Christ. This is the reason why Jesus told the devil in the desert, after being tempted, "Man shall not live by bread alone, but by every word that proceeds from the mouth of God" (Matt. 4:4). Jesus' "food" was to do the will of the Father, revealed in the Scriptures.

The Christian Church teaches that we are dependent upon these words for real life. They are our nourishment and God's instruction manual for the life He's breathed into us. They not only tell us how to live, but they demonstrate it in the Person of Christ, who is the living Word of God.

The Church teaches that the entirety of Scripture reveals the Person and work of Christ. While walking on the road to Emmaus with His disciples, Jesus "beginning at Moses and all the Prophets . . . expounded to them in all the Scriptures the things concerning Himself" (Luke 24:27). Like a photo mosaic, in which one picture is made up of many other carefully arranged smaller pictures, the Scriptures are a story mosaic, in which all the books and all the stories they contain help us to see clearly the story of God's love for us through His Son, Jesus.

Some of these stories are of people, some are the stories of nations, some tell how the world began and how it will end, some are unique and filled with poetry and wise sayings, some are letters written to a person or a church, and some are about the life and teachings of Jesus. What's important to understand is that God inspired people to write these books so that

His Son might be perfectly revealed to us. It's the revelation of human life!

We remain oriented to our destination of communion with God by being obedient to God's Word, on whom we're dependent for life. The connection between obedience and dependence is natural. The question is on what or on whom have we made ourselves dependent? Many of us obey the sources that feed our false self. We become dependent on the vices that feed and protect our ego, whether they're possessions, relationships, or titles. This kind of dependence steals from us the joy of living a life of obedience to the One for whom we were created.

God designed us to be nourished by truth. Truth leads to accurate perceptions about life, and accurate perceptions lead to healthy emotions and actions. According to the Psalmist, the righteous man is the one who meditates on this day and night: "He shall be like a tree / Planted by the rivers of water, / That brings forth its fruit in its season, / Whose leaf also shall not wither; / And whatever he does shall prosper" (Ps. 1:3).

Reading and reflecting on the Scriptures is a transformational habit that leads to a discerning obedience. When Jesus was tempted by the devil's perverse use of the Scriptures, he did not respond with blind obedience, but made discerning responses from the Scriptures. With each temptation, He replied, "It is written . . ." With these responses, the Scriptures say, "the devil . . . departed from Him" (Luke 4:13). When we ruminate on the Scriptures in our hearts and minds, we're able to challenge and take captive those thoughts and emotions that are contrary to a virtuous life.

## The Fountain of Life

The functional movements of orientation, communion, worship, and obedience are shaped within us in the context of the Church. The virtuous life that the Church offers us is the crucified and glorified life of Jesus Christ—"for in Him we live and move and have our being" (Acts 17:28). I like to illustrate these specific movements and their relationship to one another by comparing the Church to a three-tiered fountain.

The basin at the bottom of the fountain represents the synergy of efforts to *reorient* our lives to God. This is the pool of spiritual conversion from which everything else in our spiritual lives springs forth. We identify ourselves with the death and Resurrection of Jesus Christ through the waters of baptism and our being filled by the gift of the Holy Spirit. Through the transformational habits of confession, reconciliation, and spiritual direction we continually reorient our lives to communion with Him and others.

From these habits our lives naturally move to the second tier of the fountain where we seek to restore the wholeness of our God-given nature, lost through our own vices. In this basin, our humanity is restored through the natural movements that take place within community. We relearn the movements of worship, obedience, and community by gathering each Sunday with the faithful to worship God and obey the teachings of His Word. This leads us to a loving and sacrificial manner of life that always seeks the good of the other and strengthens the foundation of community. From this basin God touches our hearts through worship, the Scriptures, and His people.

These interactions direct us in two different movements: (1) they convict us of our need to reorient our lives in even deeper ways, so that parts of our lives naturally and perpetually spill back into the first basin of spiritual conversion; and (2) they lead us to *respond* to God's calling in our personal lives—the third and final tier of the fountain.

The more we embrace the love of God in our lives through worship, obedience, and community, the more we're compelled to express it through the gifts, abilities, experiences, and resources God has given us. These are to be shared inside and outside the bounds of the Church. Inside they are experienced as gifts through which we sacrifice ourselves for the edification of the Church, and outside they're acts and words of mercy that witness to the saving love of Jesus Christ.

Again, as we naturally respond to the calling of God's love in our lives we, and others, are convicted of our need for deeper surrender and spiritual conversion. The result is that the virtuous waters of life moving in this fountain are continually spilling over from one basin to the other in a perpetual sanctifying motion that leads us ever deeper into our experience of communion with God and our neighbor.

# CHAPTER SEVEN

# Giving Your Life Away

*I have found the paradox, that if you love until it hurts, there can
be no more hurt, only more love.*

—Mother Teresa[14]

WHEN I WAS IN COLLEGE, I volunteered in my church's
high school youth ministry program. On a regular
basis we did events with a sister church in the same county.
As a result I became friends with the youth pastor from that
church—Jerry Riffe.

Pastor Jerry, or PJ as we called him, served the youth of that
church for three decades. He referred to himself as a "fool for
Jesus," and he was. He was a man who stood out. If it weren't
for his Birkenstock sandals that he wore year-round, you'd
swear he was a Marine Corps drill instructor. He was tall, with
a lean and muscular build, and he always sported a tight buzz
cut. People loved him, but most (myself include) were intimi-
dated by his radical love for God. He lived a very simple life,
with intense discipline and without any pretense. He believed
and preached that the Christian struggle was won with prayer,

fasting, serving the poor, and obedience to the Scriptures. He was essentially a Baptist ascetic.

Oddly enough, it was this Protestant youth pastor who first introduced me to the writings of Mother Teresa of Calcutta. He quoted her often and emulated her life. Everywhere he went, he sought out the poor and brokenhearted. Every week PJ was to be found somewhere in the city feeding the homeless or ministering to the imprisoned. As often as he could, he took students or adults from the church with him. During school breaks, he would take the kids from his youth group to Mexico, where they would serve the poorest of the poor.

On one of his trips, he fell asleep at the wheel and rolled the bus down a hillside, killing one of his own daughters. He spent that night alone in a Mexican prison cell. He said it changed his life. I'm not sure how his life was changed, but I know God used him to change mine.

Pastor Jerry's love for the poor affected the entire course of my life. His example and the writings of Mother Teresa compelled me to take the Scriptures seriously. The nineteenth-century Danish philosopher Søren Kierkegaard wrote:

The matter is quite simple. The Bible is very easy to understand. But we Christians are a bunch of scheming swindlers. We pretend to be unable to understand it because we know very well that the minute we understand, we are obliged to act accordingly. Take any words in the New Testament and forget anything except pledging yourself to act accordingly. "My God," you will say, "if I do that my whole life will be ruined. How would I ever get on in the world?"[15]

Over the past decade, God has "ruined" my life as I have journeyed with students to inner cities and third-world countries. For years I was able to ignore or allegorize away the difficult passages of Scripture concerning poverty, but now I'm haunted by them because they have faces. I've discovered that the Christian life can only be fulfilled in sacrificial acts of love. Everything else is just talk. Love is our human vocation, and it is most perfectly revealed on the Cross.

From the beginning, it was God's intention and will that His entire human creation would share His divine life and blessing—that all of His creation would call upon Him as Father and God. Of course, man rebelled, and all of humanity was fragmented—this is the story of the first eleven chapters of Genesis, which culminate in the chaos of the Tower of Babel. In the twelfth chapter, God speaks to Abraham concerning his vocation. He tells him to "get out" so He can make him "a blessing" (Gen. 12:1–2). God tells Abraham, "in you all the families of the earth shall be blessed" (Gen. 12:3). Six more times in the book of Genesis this affirmation is repeated. God was calling Abraham and his descendants, Israel, to their neglected human vocation—witnessing to the love and goodness of God.

In the final book of the Scriptures, Revelation, the author records a heavenly vision of "a great multitude which no one could number, of all nations, tribes, peoples, and tongues, standing before the throne and before the Lamb" (Rev. 7:9). This heavenly scene is the reason why each of us was created with a natural movement toward God. This vision is the fulfillment of God's creation in Genesis chapter one. We were created to be gathered around the throne of God in eternal communion with Him and one another.

Israel's existence was not a special birthright separate from the other nations. God didn't care more for Israel as a nation than He did for the others. Israel was God's vehicle to fulfill and actualize His love for all people. Israel's election was made by God with a special purpose: "I have known [Israel], in order that he may command his children and his household after him, that they keep the way of the LORD, to do righteousness and justice" (Gen. 18:19).

This righteousness and justice to which the book of Genesis refers was supposed to be the missional ethic and character of Israel's vocation. The Scriptures say that God set them apart as a "kingdom of priests" (Ex. 19:6). Their role was to bring the presence of God's love and forgiveness to all the nations. For this reason, God prescribed the Law in order that Israel might live differently and become a light to the nations—drawing all people to Himself. The prophet Isaiah foretold that Israel was "To open blind eyes, / To bring out prisoners from the prison, / Those who sit in darkness from the prison house" (Is. 42:7). Israel was given a divine mission of service and love. If they carried out their mission, the surrounding nations would notice and say, "Surely this great nation *is* a wise and understanding people" (Deut. 4:6).

## Sacrifice

In the spring of 1988, just a year before the Romanian Revolution, I joined a group of college friends traveling to Bucharest to minister to the underground Church. At the time, the country was still under the iron grip of the Communist dictator, Nicolae Ceaușescu. His brutal and rigid reign was arguably the most infamous regime in the Soviet bloc. Dissent was never tolerated. Most of the people starved, waiting in long lines for their monthly rations of flour, sugar, butter, and other living necessities.

When we arrived at the airport, each one of us was carrying multiple suitcases stuffed with hidden Bibles. We had practiced, over and over again, what to say if we were questioned by security. As we queued up, soldiers studied our passports while others pillaged through our bags. My prayers were frantic, and I was frightened by "what if" scenarios. The entire experience seemed to slow down time. "How can these soldiers not see all the Bibles stuffed throughout our luggage?" I worried. Out of a group of nearly twenty, they confiscated only one or two of our bags—and without any reprisal. It seemed like a miracle. However, on the other side of security their strategy became more transparent, as we were picked up and tailed by government officials.

Once we were settled in our carefully surveilled hotel, the leadership of our group began making secretive arrangements to meet our Christian hosts. In a crowded public market we met our contact and agreed upon a time and location to meet the underground Church. Later that evening, we pulled up to a large and vacant parking lot. There were only one or two cars besides ours.

We entered a large building and were immediately escorted

into a private office where we were introduced to the pastoral leadership of the Church. The men had radiant faces and were obviously overjoyed at our visit. After several minutes of pleasantries, service details, and prayer, we followed the pastors through a set of double doors and into an auditorium literally packed to the walls with hundreds of Christians waiting for our arrival. "Did all of these people walk here?" I thought to myself.

The service went on for hours, and many stood the entire time because of limited seating. It finally ended when all of the lights in the building abruptly went out. Almost instantaneously, everyone filed out of the building. It was hard to tell if we should be worried. Was electricity being rationed like the food, or had the government discovered our meeting? Our team was escorted into a small candlelit room with a banquet table at the center, filled with the finest homemade pastries and baked goods I have ever seen or tasted. At the expense of their own families, the women of the Church had saved their monthly rations to prepare a feast for us. I remember their faces—brighter than the candles! Their sacrifice was pure joy.

When the medicine of the Church begins to heal our broken lives, it will naturally be demonstrated in sacrificial movements. We will joyfully contribute our God-given gifts, experiences, and resources to those in need, most especially to those who cannot repay us. To the person enslaved by their selfish appetites, sacrifice is painful and rarely considered; but to the person being freed through the healing medicines of the Church, giving becomes a way of life and a way of honoring Jesus' sacrifice on the Cross.

In the midst of real struggle and persecution, these women were fulfilling their human vocation through the smallest gestures of love and hospitality. When love takes root in our hearts, it will find even the smallest cracks in which to bloom. Thérèse of Lisieux wrote, "Miss no single opportunity of making some small sacrifice, here by a smiling look, there by a kindly word; always doing the smallest right and doing it all for love."[16] It is these small, daily gestures—unnoticeable to most, sometimes even to us—that evidence the real metamorphosis of the human heart.

Israel failed to fulfill its vocational calling. Instead of becoming a light to the nations, they became like them. Like Adam and Eve, they didn't trust God. Instead, they desired the leadership of a king, like the surrounding nations had. And like Adam and Eve, again, their desires eventually led them into exile.

It's within this context that God sends His only Son, Jesus, to fulfill what Israel was destined to do in and through Him alone. In the fourth chapter of Luke, Jesus reads in the synagogue a prophecy concerning Himself: "'The Spirit of the LORD *is* upon Me, / Because He has anointed Me / To preach the gospel to *the* poor; / He has sent Me to heal the brokenhearted, / To proclaim liberty to *the* captives / And recovery of sight to *the* blind, / To set at liberty those who are oppressed'" (Luke 4:18). Sacrificial love is the light of the world and is most perfectly expressed by Jesus hanging on the Cross. Jesus says, "And I, if I am lifted up from the earth, will draw all *peoples* to Myself" (John 12:32). In this act, Jesus fulfills the mission of His Father to be a "light to the Gentiles" (Is. 49:6).

After Jesus is raised from the dead, He commissions His disciples with the same word with which His Father commissioned Abraham: "Go therefore and make disciples of all the nations, baptizing them in the name of the Father and of the Son and of the Holy Spirit, teaching them to observe all things that I have commanded you; and lo, I am with you always, *even to the end of the age*" (Matt. 28:19–20). With these instructions, the Church is handed the baton of Israel's mission. Jesus sends His Spirit to anoint and fill the twelve disciples with His power, commissioning them to become the hands and feet of His love to a lost and broken world.

In the spring of 2007, I took a group of college students to the Dominican Republic to work in an orphanage called Jackie's House. Jackie and her husband Ernesto take in the children whose exceedingly poor parents can't afford to raise them. Many of the children come from one community in particular—some call it Trash Mountain.

One afternoon Jackie and Ernesto invited us to join them on their visit to this community. We rode with them on dusty roads to the outskirts of Santo Domingo, where the city placed its dump. As we drove up to the gates, armed soldiers carrying assault rifles met us. "Why in the world would you need armed soldiers at a city dump?" I thought to myself.

After a lengthy conversation and a financial bribe we were allowed to enter. For nearly a half hour we walked on sunbaked roads, escorted by soldiers, while dump trucks raced past us. Each of us wore bandanas to keep the dust and stench from our nostrils. As we crested the hill we'd been climbing for some time, we saw a foothill in the distance, maybe three stories tall. It looked like it was moving. At first, I thought it might be the waves of heat rising from the parched ground, but as I got closer I realized that the movement resembled ants climbing over their mound. I leaned forward and squinted my eyes together to bring the image into clearer focus. After several seconds I was finally able to make out the movement—it was people climbing and digging through a giant mound of trash. Whatever I was expecting, it wasn't this!

We hiked around the backside of Trash Mountain and walked up the ramp used by the garbage trucks to leave their haul. At the top, women and children sorted recyclables for money, and bulldozers pushed piles of refuse over the edge onto the climbers below. Few wore shoes, and most were darkened by the sun and dirt in which they labored. One of the soldiers remarked with disdain that during the previous week a man was stabbed to death over a bag of Cheetos. Trash Mountain was a desperate and dangerous place. I couldn't help but reflect on how these people had become like animals in a pack, scavenging for food and fighting among themselves for survival. This was a forsaken place with forgotten people.

Later in the afternoon we visited the village situated at the edge of the dump where so many of the children at Jackie's House hailed from. Narrow dirt streets were lined with shanty dwellings made of materials from the dump. Children wandered naked through the alleyways, darting in and out of doorways made out of bedsheets. We met the maimed and the diseased. Some of them looked indifferent, some angry, but no one looked glad to see us. We were just another group of do-gooders wandering through their zoo of survival gawking at their friends and family like caged animals.

We followed one group of adults carrying buckets to the town well. When we arrived, we found men and women holding a variety of containers underneath a rusted, algae-covered pipe protruding from underneath the street. It trickled a murky liquid into a putrid creek below. "Invisible" was the only word that came to mind. "These people are absolutely invisible," I thought.

## Witness

Jesus' ministry was powerful because He saw people—no one was invisible to Him. He saw the woman caught in adultery and the hypocritical hearts of the ones ready to throw stones; He saw a Samaritan woman and the pain of her past relationships; He saw the grieving heart of a woman who had lost her son; He saw the desperation of countless others whose ailments left them without hope or community; and finally, when hanging on the Cross, He saw us and said, "Father, forgive them, for they do not know what they do" (Luke 23:34).

Witnessing or seeing the reality of life all around us is another fundamental movement of our human nature. Many of us really don't want to see or know what's going on in the lives of the people with whom we interact daily, much less the world. It's too painful, and we don't want to be accountable for things that feel overwhelming to us. Willful blindness is a coping mechanism, but it has a downside—it shrinks our hearts.

Jesus, quoting the prophet Isaiah, said that some people have closed their eyes, so their eyes cannot see and their hearts cannot understand.

We wrongly assume that our hearts cannot bear the weight of reality. How many parents have worried unnecessarily that they wouldn't be able to love their second child as much as their first? Our hearts were designed with elasticity for the other. We are most human when we take others seriously and seek to embrace, however feebly, the reality of their lives.

For nearly a decade I had the privilege of leading students into the nation's largest inner cities and exposing them to the complexities of domestic poverty. Those were the most rewarding years of my ministry. The highlight of every trip was our Meal Search. I would split the students into small groups of two or three and give each person three dollars to purchase a meal. Additionally, I gave each group an extra three dollars to invite a homeless person to eat with them. Their instructions were to find out as much about that person as possible.

The group reactions were always so predictable, I could have scripted each experience. Inevitably, the students would leave sheepishly, even frightened at the thought of interacting with a homeless person. However, when they returned you could see their smiles and enthusiasm a block away! When all of us gathered to debrief the experience, students couldn't wait to share their personal stories. It was always an "aha moment" for them—people are people no matter what the context! All of us have parents, friends, dreams, interests, disappointments, and loves. The human experience is a common experience, and although the contexts might be different, the basic elements (love, suffering, relationships, hopes, etc.) of each storyline are the same.

At the conclusion of our debriefs, I would always ask the students the same question: "How would you feel if the people who passed you by every day couldn't look you in the eyes?" There was always a reflective pause followed by the same responses: "horrible," "unloved," "worthless," "inhuman," etc. And with that question, nothing more needed to be said. The students left the inner cities not only understanding the importance of discovering Christ in the poor, but also seeing the emotional and spiritual poverty in their own homes and friendships.

God has given each of us physical, emotional, and spiritual eyes to witness and respond to the reality of His creation. This is the fundamental building block of our relationship with Him. Adam and Eve failed to see creation for what it really was—a revelation of God's love and goodness. Instead, they saw and interpreted everything relative to themselves. They were duped into believing that life was all about them. The truth is that our life is always found in the other. Our human vocation is fulfilled, and so are we, when we live in the present with the intention of discovering and witnessing God's presence in every person, place, and circumstance.

It's only when we live in reality that we can truly serve and love the other. We must take people seriously—regardless of their age and circumstance. We must be willing to take the time and emotional energy to see people for who they really are and the situations in which they really live. We must seek to love real people, not caricatures—"for he who does not love his brother whom he has seen, how can he love God whom he has not seen?" (1 John 4:20).

# CHAPTER EIGHT

# Momentary Habits

*A nail is driven out by another nail; habit is overcome by habit.*
—Erasmus

T HE CHURCH IS ALWAYS A HOSPITAL, but sometimes it feels like an asylum. Over a decade ago, I had an experience with someone in church authority that felt like a scene out of *One Flew over the Cuckoo's Nest*. I can't go into detail, but it was the most surreal and humiliating moment of my life—like a bizarre dream sequence. The episode left me nearly blinded by rage and seriously questioning whether I could continue my ministry in the Church.

About a year later, my marriage and my pastorate ended. While I take full responsibility for shipwrecking both, I would be lying if I said that the collective experiences of my ministry, including the one recounted above, didn't take a toll on my marriage and on myself. For three years I wandered through a malaise of anger and pain. Every time I came into contact with church leadership I had a psychosomatic reaction; I literally wanted to vomit. I longed to be connected again to the Church, but I felt repulsed by the thought of its leadership.

Finally I came to the realization that I had to grow up, and so did my faith. How ironic for a man who had spent most of his working life in the Church. My real hurdle in coming back to the Church was figuring out how to manage my raging feelings of anger, self-pity, and anxiety. It was easy to point my finger at other people and situations, but I was the one who was harboring the past. I had become a reservoir of pain, and I was slowly poisoning myself with bitterness. I felt my relationship with God being choked out by my inability to deal with the barrage of feelings and thoughts that were almost always racing through my head and heart.

I eventually found a path back through practicing what I call *momentary habits*. I'm learning to restore my sanity and intimacy with God through centering prayer, mindful breathing, gratitude, and letting go. These are daily habits we can practice in our minds to bring us into, and transform, the present moment.

Each day the Holy Spirit seeks to use the events and relationships of our lives to sanctify our humanity. We have the opportunity to cooperate with Him and say "yes" to His therapeutic activities in our lives. But all therapy involves some level of pain or discomfort, and, too often, we fail to see the redemptive value of this pain and suffering. Not only do they lead us to discover more about ourselves and the reality around us, but they can also purge our lives from the unessential distractions and vices that keep us from growing into the likeness of our Creator.

Jesus shows us that suffering can be redemptive when it's accepted in love and obedience to God. The pain and suffering in this fallen world were never part of God's plan for humanity, but He never abandons us. His love swallows every evil and distortion and transforms them into possibilities of resurrection. Each day we experience a myriad of pains, frustrations, and discomforts, all of which hold real transformative power. Each of these moments pivot on our response—our resistance or acceptance.

It's natural to avoid pain and suffering, but it isn't natural to resist the loving Providence of God. God didn't will the pain, suffering, and death of humanity, but He does will a way through it. In this fallen world, resurrection comes through suffering. It is the primary path in which we travel from the image of God to the likeness of God. It's on the Cross of suffering that Jesus demonstrates His love and obedience to the Father. He agonizes in the Garden of Gethsemane but accepts His Father's providential will.

Our sufferings have the same potential. In every fallen relationship and situation, God extends the grace of His Resurrection. We can accept the gift of His grace with gratitude like Mary. She let go of her anxieties and fears and surrendered herself to the loving will of God: "Let it be to me according to your word" (Luke 1:38). With these words, Mary opens the doors of her heart to the grace of God. These are timeless, transformative moments when our faith in God opens us up to the possibilities of real freedom. We passively experience the brokenness of life but actively surrender ourselves to the grace of God.

As we discussed in chapter three, our minds are the battlefield in which our humanity is won or lost. Through sin our minds have become unruly, wandering, and self-governing. Paul, in his letter to the Roman church, says, "be transformed by the renewing of your mind" (Rom. 12:2). Paul understood that this organ controls our moral behavior. Without willful direction and correction, our minds wander endlessly through the fields of our emotional anxieties and fears.

An ongoing study at Harvard University reveals the emotional cost of a wandering mind. The initial results of this study were published in *Science* magazine in an article entitled, "A Wandering Mind Is an Unhappy Mind." The opening sentence to the article is profound: "Unlike other animals, human beings spend a lot of time thinking about what is not going on around them . . ." The article goes on to say that this condition appears to be the "default mode of operation" for most people, and that we regularly contemplate "events that happened in the past, might happen in the future, or will never happen at all."

In other words, we struggle to live in the present reality. We are more comfortable racing back and forth between the past and the present because we unconsciously believe that we can control it through discursive reasoning or inner dialogues. We rewrite the history of our past experiences and relationships with creative new interpretations and fend off future suffering through imaginative dialogues with people with whom we feel particularly vulnerable. According to the study, however, mind-wandering "was generally the cause, and not merely the consequence, of unhappiness."[17] How ironic that the most natural thing we reach for in our toolbox of coping mechanisms is also the most emotionally costly.

If a wandering mind produces unhappiness, why don't we spend more time in the present moment? The answer is simple. Our broken humanity has lost its natural intuition and no longer knows what to do with the present moment. The mind is designed by God to be active. It is the organ He gave us to be co-creators with Him. With our minds we learn, solve, and strategize. In the case of the past or the future, our minds race endlessly to solve the problems of our anxieties and fears.

With the present moment, however, our minds are confused as to what should be done. Unless there is a clear and imposing objective, our minds naturally speed past the present moment toward the areas of greatest pleasure or pain. In the case of pleasure, the mind races to clear the path or duplicate the experience; and in the case of pain, it seeks to alleviate the stress and discomfort of psychological/emotional disequilibrium—they are both distorted survival mechanisms.

In order to fully recover our humanity, we must regain control over our minds. The first step in this realignment operation is to help our minds stay in the present moment. In the Harvard study referred to earlier, researchers studied the correlation between mind-wandering and twenty-two different activities derived from the reconstruction of a typical person's day. The study revealed that people's minds wander regularly in every activity except one—sex. Sex provides a big enough "why" to stay in the present moment. Our minds stay anchored to the experiences of greatest pleasure and pain. This is the reason why the vices are such strong forces in our daily lives—they are passionate extensions of our personal experience with pleasure and pain. They reflect our desire to duplicate pleasure and our determination to avoid pain.

Our communion with God, and our ongoing salvation, can only happen in the present moment, but our active minds struggle to stay there when they are not filled with an experience of pleasure or pain rivaling the experiences of our past. Unfortunately, few of us have had spiritual experiences of pleasure that rival our most intimate human encounters, and many of us have had painful religious experiences that remain with us today. In order to train our minds to remain in the present, we must help them find paths back to the present moment, and this requires great patience.

When I was in seminary, my favorite professor would tell us regularly that our thoughts and emotions were like birds. He would say, "You can't control them flying over your head, but you can prevent them from nesting there." Trying to wrestle and fight our thoughts and emotions is a losing battle. Most of the time we only exacerbate them. Our goal should be to keep them from nesting. We can never know for certain where our thoughts and feelings come from, but a simple prayer asking for Jesus' mercy can reorient our minds, bring us into the present moment, and reconnect us with reality.

## Centering Prayer

Some authors would suggest that you should manufacture a big enough *why* or goal to capture and keep your mind in the present moment. This seems unnatural to me and more like mental gymnastics. As our broken identities heal, the "why" we are seeking will eventually surface and become self-evident. Until then, when you become aware that your mind has wandered, simply ask Christ to descend into the depths of your anxieties, fears, and vices and fill them with His light and truth. You can simply pray, "Lord Jesus, fill this situation/relationship with Your mercy."

In this way, we "[bring] every thought into captivity to the obedience of Christ" (2 Cor. 10:5). If He can descend into death, then He can certainly descend into the dark pits of our wandering minds. These, after all, are the places we need His healing touch. These are the distorted and imaginary places that drive our broken beliefs, perceptions, feelings, and actions. These are the places that need His light. Scolding or beating ourselves up about our wandering minds won't help. It is a reality of our broken, human condition—to believe anything else is prideful delusion. When we say a simple prayer for the Lord's mercy we gently bring ourselves back into the present moment with our minds centered on Him.

These brief prayers require only the cry of our hearts and can be shot like arrows into the very presence of God. Christians have been practicing these short prayers, in conjunction with their normal daily prayers, for two millennia. In the beginning, these prayers came from the Psalms. One such prayer that was used frequently was adapted from the seventieth Psalm: *"Make haste, O God, to deliver me! / Make haste to help me, O LORD!"* (Ps. 70:1). Christians used these short prayers in their daily life to keep their attention focused on the Kingdom of God. They can be repeated, with feeling, over and over while doing just about any activity. A popular practice in Eastern Christianity is "The Jesus Prayer." The prayer is simply: "Lord Jesus Christ, Son of God, have mercy upon me a sinner." Sometimes it is shortened even further: "Lord Jesus Christ, have mercy on me."

These are the kinds of prayers that are often combined with the use of rosary beads or a prayer rope. People use these tangible objects to help them stay focused on the moment and the task of prayer. Each time their fingers move over a bead or knot, they say the short prayer. The exact words are less important than the motivation and feeling of the heart from which they spring forth. The danger, of course, is vain repetition. These short prayers are not magical incantations; they are expressions of our deepest desire to be healed. If they come from this place in our hearts, then they can help us reorient toward God.

These prayers allow us to obey Jesus' command: "when you pray, go into your room, and when you have shut your door, pray to your Father who *is* in the secret *place*" (Matt. 6:6). These prayers are always accessible to us and allow us to pray anywhere, even in the most difficult of situations. This was the kind of prayer Fr. Roman practiced while in prison. In his book, he wrote, "In those difficult moments I confess that I started to recite the Jesus Prayer and practiced it intensely. Only then was I able to discover how beautiful the interior life of man is."[18] We, like Fr. Roman, can discover that God is always present in the "inner room" of our hearts.

This is the reason why so many of the early Christian writers instructed us to shut the door of our minds and pray with our minds in our hearts. The heart is a still place and only exists in the present moment. It is the holy temple of God's dwelling. Thoughts do not race through the heart. It is a place of truth, clarity, discernment, and communion. Defining it is easy— accessing it, however, takes real effort and requires us to realign our broken natures.

There is a natural hierarchy to the human person. While the mind is the pilot of the body, it was never intended to be self-governed. The mind must be inspired and directed by God's Spirit who dwells in our hearts. The nest of our mind is our heart—the only place where God dwells. With patience and persistence we can begin to train our minds to rest in this holy place.

## Mindful Breathing

One of the historic methods practiced in this training is mindful breathing. In other words, paying specific attention to your breath—your inhalation and your exhalation. The act of breathing is a gift from God. The Scriptures record that He "breathed into [our] nostrils the breath of life" (Gen. 2:7). Every time we pay attention to this breath entering and leaving our bodies, we witness the breath of God coursing through us.

By being mindful of this, we are reminded that there is no life apart from Him.

The simple exercise of paying attention to your breath brings all of your attention and focus into the present moment. It's an effective way of shutting off your racing mind and descending into the stillness of your heart. When we practice mindful breathing, we lay aside discursive reasoning and every other kind of mental gymnastics. The goal is simply to reestablish our communion with God and to be still in His presence.

Initially, it's easy, but staying in the present moment can be very difficult. Sometimes I will count my breaths in order to remain in the moment. Once I'm able to calm my mind down and settle into an even rhythm of inhalation and exhalation, I replace my counting with the Jesus Prayer: "Lord Jesus Christ, Son of God, have mercy on me." Our goal is not to empty our minds, like the Buddhists, but rather to fill them with the presence of God so we can commune with Him.

This can be practiced as a daily meditative exercise or throughout the day as your life permits. The goal is to keep our minds engaged in the present moment and to prevent them from racing off to imaginative dialogues or rehearsals of the past. As you practice this more and more, you will feel a growing peacefulness in your life and an increased awareness of your surroundings. These are the first fruits of real human freedom. It is a return to the stillness of the Garden of Eden, where mankind was created to live in the presence of God and marvel at His provision and love.

## Gratitude

With time, our growing awareness of God's presence will give birth to a thankful heart, but gratitude is a discipline that can be practiced regardless of our feelings. It is a willful and prayerful affirmation of God's love and control in our lives. When we say "thank you" to God, we confess the mystery of His providential will and the shortsightedness of our anxieties and fears. My favorite poem is "The Guest House," by the thirteenth-century Persian poet, Rumi. In it, Rumi describes how a grateful heart can produce a dispassionate mind.

### The Guest House

This being human is a guest house.
Every morning a new arrival.

A joy, a depression, a meanness,
some momentary awareness comes as an unexpected visitor.

Welcome and entertain them all!
Even if they're a crowd of sorrows,
who violently sweep your house
empty of its furniture,
still, treat each guest honorably.
He may be clearing you out
for some new delight.

The dark thought, the shame, the malice,
meet them at the door laughing,
and invite them in.

Be grateful for whoever comes,
because each has been sent
as a guide from beyond.[19]

At first, Rumi's description of welcoming and inviting in our thoughts and feelings may appear to contradict the idea of never allowing these to nest in our heads. But Rumi isn't suggesting we initiate the invitation; after all, these visitors are unexpected. Instead, Rumi uses the metaphor of hospitality to underscore the importance of observing what these visitors reveal in us. It's true that some of our guests are enemies in disguise, but if they are treated with force they acquire even more power. Carl Jung argued that "what you resist not only persists, but will grow in size."[20] In most cases, when we try not to think about something, the thought becomes cemented even more strongly into our consciousness.

We can welcome our thoughts and feelings with gratitude, even laugh at them in humility, recognizing that even the worst guest has value. If we observe carefully, each of them has something to teach us. As innkeepers, our job is to treat each with respect and make certain that none take up permanent residence.

The key is not to be surprised by the emotions and thoughts that storm through our heads. Instead, we should expect them with humility. Why wouldn't we? Most people have unconsciously loosed their minds to wander and explore every past pain and every future possibility. Our minds have been given free reign over our feelings, perceptions, and beliefs. When we begin to limit their activities, we should expect great resistance.

During these times we can simply pray, "Thank you, Lord, for Your loving will and for what I cannot see." The recovery of our humanity is lived in this dynamic tension—the tension of God's eternal will and our earthly perceptions. Most of us buckle under the uncertainties of not knowing everything or being in complete control. The unconscious and unspoken assumption is that we know best and that God is the great vending machine in the sky. This is not redemption, though—this is just more of the same broken trajectory! If we want to live differently, we have to begin acting differently.

Gratitude is an intentional expression that can drive the alignment of our feelings, perceptions, and beliefs. Gratitude anticipates God's love and provision in our lives, even when we don't feel or see it. It nudges us to see past the immediate tension and to release our desire to control everything in our lives.

## Letting Go

When we let go of the delusion of control, we surrender ourselves to dependence on God—the normal and natural state of every human being. This is a very uncomfortable feeling for most of us. Our minds want to solve their own problems. They want to bypass discomfort and tension. They spin, looking for creative solutions and ways out of uncertainty.

Our broken minds are the reason we struggle to let go. They have only one objective: to preserve our broken identity at all costs. We're scared to discover, or for others to discover, that who we are and what we do is not enough. Our minds actively try to protect our egos and solve problems that they helped create through their myopic and self-centered perspective. This is why we must shut them down through mindful breathing and return to the center of our hearts, praying, "Lord Jesus, descend into my anxieties and strengthen my faith."

The Scriptures advise: "Trust in the LORD with all your heart, / And lean not on your own understanding" (Prov. 3:5). This admonition takes us back to the Genesis account where Adam and Eve fell prey to their own reasoning. Genesis says that Eve "saw that the tree *was* good for food, that it *was* pleasant to the eyes, and a tree desirable to make *one* wise" (Gen. 3:6). They both gave into the temptation of questioning God's love and provision for them. Ultimately they believed God was withholding something from them that they could attain on their own. Instead of finding wisdom, they discovered the shame and bondage of their own understanding.

Our minds were not created to act independently of God, but to co-create. When they are fixed on the depths of God's love and provision, they are set free to creatively and faithfully engage with any and every context. Our deepest mental obstacle is the difficulty of truly believing that God is our Father and will not forsake or abandon us. Mindful breathing puts a stop to all the vain and crazy thoughts screaming for love and acceptance. It brings us back to the reality of the breath and life that God lovingly gave to us. And in these moments of clarity we have the opportunity to let go of the lies that drive our anxieties and anchor us to suffering.

The act of letting go is a step toward living in reality—seeing and interacting with people and situations for who and what they really are. Our vices can blind us in so many ways. It's easy for us to make people into monsters and situations into hopeless tragedies. Our human freedom can easily be lost in this delusion, and we can become slaves to our own understanding and reasoning. Stopping our racing minds, centering them in the stillness of our hearts, and letting go of our impulse to control and solve everything are the first steps toward living a life filled with freedom and virtue.

# CHAPTER NINE

# Living in Reality

*We must speak of reality from the perspective of the Gospel,
through the prism of the Cross.*

—Fr. Thomas Hopko

O n Monday, April 16, 2007, I was catching up with my
staff during a normal morning conference call when one
of them asked if I had heard about the shooting at Virginia
Tech. At the time, I was directing a nationwide campus ministry program that supported 270 local university chapters across
the US and Canada. In a bit of shock, I immediately searched
our local chapter database. My heart sank when I saw Virginia
Tech in Blacksburg, Virginia on the list. In that moment, the
feelings and memories of 9/11 rushed back through me. Self-
ishly, I thought to myself, "not again—not me." I knew in my
role there was no way I could avoid responding to the crisis, but
this was a chapter of my life I did not want to revisit.

As soon as we ended the conference call, I turned on the TV
to watch the coverage. My chest tightened as I watched familiar

scenes of first responders, yellow tape, and victims on stretchers. I knew I was headed back into a world of unspeakable human suffering. Over the course of the day, I stayed glued to the news and the growing body count. The entire campus had become a crime scene and was in lockdown. I knew it was going to be difficult for my staff to get an accurate report of our local chapter there. I waited for the weekend and flew into Roanoke.

Despite the light snowfall and colder temperatures earlier in the week, it was a beautiful, sunny day in southwest Virginia. The airport was quiet and relatively empty. There was nothing to indicate that just three days earlier, and only forty miles away, the deadliest shooting in US history had occurred. I grabbed my rental car and headed west on the hour-long trip to Blacksburg. Spring seemed oblivious to the mourning state. The redbuds were in full bloom on the rolling hills along Interstate 81.

With each mile the scenery blurred, and my mind became hypnotized by my anxieties. I knew I was entering into the war zone of human emotion and pain all over again. The initial reports from our local chapter were promising; apparently none of our students or faculty had been in Norris Hall that morning. But I knew from 9/11, that made very little difference. Trauma of that magnitude finds a way into the human psyche.

I had never before visited Virginia Tech. It's a gorgeous campus spread out over 2,600 acres. Most of the buildings are constructed with a colorful limestone they call Hokie Stone. When I arrived on campus, I checked in with the university administration and was badged as a visiting chaplain.

As a part of our organization's ministerial response, I asked three other chaplains to join me. One was a police officer from Buffalo, New York, and the other two were pastors from the Boston metropolitan area. All three men had extensive training and experience as first responders. Two of them had even served in the aftermath of Hurricane Katrina. We met up at the Newman Center and planned out the following day's agenda. Our plan was to meet with the local chapter, administer a post-traumatic stress inventory, and conduct a formal incident debriefing. It felt a little stiff, but all of us knew from past experience that this would open up plenty of informal opportunities to help those who really needed it.

After dinner, we headed back to campus to join the community in their mourning. Norris Hall, where the shooting took place, is located on the northwest side of the Drillfield—an enormous oval grass field at the center of campus. The student body had constructed a makeshift memorial there, directly in front of Burruss Hall, the main administrative building. When we visited that evening, there were thirty-three memorials arranged in a semicircle. The sun had set, and the memorials were glowing from hundreds of candles. Each of the memorials was identifiable by an American flag, a Hokie stone, and a temporary name plaque. All of them were littered with flowers, candles, stuffed animals, and notes from loved ones.

Slowly, I worked my way from one end to the other. I felt like I was at the family assistance shelter all over again. Tears rolled down my face as I perused the pictures and notes from family and friends. Each of the victim's faces was so young. In my faithlessness, it was impossible for me to look at these faces without wondering what kind of future was lost with each life. When I reached the last memorial, there were no pictures— just a name, a candle, some flowers, and a note. The name read: Seung-Hui Cho. What?! The students included the shooter among the victims? Stunned by his inclusion, I reached down to pick up the solitary note. It read:

> To Cho:
> I am a Hokie.
> You cannot strip me of that, or
> My love, my passion or my truth.
> My innocence is mine on the cross
> And you cannot have it.
> You will not now nor ever
> Have power over me.
> The truth is I miss you.
> I wish that I could have shown you
> His love, His passion, His truth.
> It has set me Free
> And I wish that I could share that with you.
> I missed you.
> I am sorry.
> So I must tell you now:
> Even though you took innocent lives;
> Even though you tried to put fear in our hearts;
> Even though I hurt to the core;
> Even though my eyes are tired of crying;
> Even though my campus, my home, will never be the same . . .
> I forgive you.
> And I love you.
> Erica

I sat in a deep squat, motionless, staring blankly at the note, and lost in thought. I didn't know Erica, but I was dumbfounded by her clarity. Not only did she recognize Cho as a victim of a different sort, but she also admitted personal responsibility—"I missed you. I'm sorry."

Over the next couple of days I came to realize that Erica's letter was not an anomaly. One of the signs I saw on campus read, "32 gone, because 1 was lost." There was a very palpable spirit of compassion and forgiveness on campus. Cho was not an outsider. He was seen as a troubled member of the Hokie family. I couldn't help but compare this experience to my time at Ground Zero, where the emotional tone was steeped in anger and revenge.

Erica's letter was later posted on my friend's blog. One of his readers posted a response, calling the letter "easy forgiveness." I don't know about that, nor do I think it's my place to judge. What I do know is that Erica's letter demonstrated real insight into a terribly complex tragedy.

It's easy to be black and white in moments of such raw emotion, but Erica's letter was dispassionate. As a result she discerned *all* of the truths of the situation. Besides the obvious fact that Cho murdered the innocent lives of her fellow students, Erica recognized the other side of the coin as well. She saw thirty-three victims, not thirty-two. She recognized that Cho had been "missed," even by herself. And most importantly, she recognized that love and forgiveness were not something anyone could ever steal from her. Erica's letter was a memorial within a memorial. It was a symbol of the human virtue and clarity that come from a dispassionate spirit. Hers was a truly human and virtuous response.

## The Virtues

"Human virtue" should not be an oxymoron. From a Christian perspective, the words should be synonymous. The virtuous life is the only life God ever intended humans to have. While the life we live each day is our "reality," many of our experiences are far from true or real. Instead they are often an odd intersection of distorted realities and delusional perspectives. The only way we can genuinely live in reality is by discovering and surrendering to the natural movement toward God within each of us. The more this movement takes root in our lives, the more we are able to contemplate the nature of God and His creation. Our contemplation produces within us a response of awe, gratitude and surrender, which leads to deeper contemplation and defines the never-ending cycle of our communion with Him.

Through sin and death, humanity's natural structure and capacity for the virtuous life was paralyzed, but in and through Christ's crucified and glorified humanity, we look forward to a new Eden and a life of freedom. In Christ we find our true human identity and potential. In Him we have the power to bury our vices and return to the natural movements of our human nature.

In chapter three we discussed the "logic" of our vices and the suffering that accompanies them. All of us experience intolerable feelings or situations that we want to resolve. In an effort to find emotional or psychological equilibrium, we look for ways of controlling our "reality." The result is a series of broken but connected reactions that harm others and ourselves.

At the root of every vice is a lie, a distortion of the truth. On the other hand, those activities rooted in truth produce virtue. The eight virtues corresponding to the eight vices are self-control, purity, charity, peacefulness, spiritual mourning, zeal, modesty, and humility. These virtues are the natural expressions of our willful desires that the vices unnaturally pervert.

Desire or passion is a normal aspect of the human soul and reflects God's image. God gave us desire to drive the natural movements of our human nature. When this self-determination works in harmony with our God-given nature, it results in virtue and freedom; when it works against our nature, it ends in vice and bondage. Real life is experienced when we say "yes" to those activities that reflect our cooperation with God's will.

In general, God's will is expressed in those fundamental movements we've already discussed, which are captured in the Lord's Prayer: divine orientation, communion with God, worship, communion with mankind, obedience, sacrifice, suffering, and witness. These movements reflect the reality of our God-given design and destiny. They are both the fruit and the origin of the eight classical virtues, and, to the extent that we embrace them in our lives, we live in truth and reality.

### Self-Control

The life God gave us is good. We are created in His image and have the capacity to grow into an ever-deepening communion with Him and others. And while the world we live in is broken, everything God created is inherently good. Our virtues and our vices are the result of how we interact with this God-given goodness. The virtuous life begins with the fundamental truth and conviction that God loves us and can be trusted to provide for us.

In the beginning, God's provision for mankind is illustrated by a beautiful garden full of everything pleasurable to the senses. The experience of pleasure was intended to accentuate our awareness of the gifts of God's goodness and to strengthen our communion of love with Him.

The fruit of pleasure is sweet and life-sustaining when it is rooted in the conviction that everything good comes from God above. The problem occurs when we are tempted to believe that God cannot be trusted and that we must create our own world of goodness, seeking pleasure as being desirable in and of itself. This kind of pleasure is initially sweet, but it ends with a bitter aftertaste that brings death. For this reason, there was a fast in the Garden from the very beginning: "Of every tree of the garden you may freely eat; but of the tree of the knowledge of good and evil you shall not eat, for in the day that you eat of it you shall surely die" (Gen. 2:16–17).

The virtue of self-control begins with a deep conviction of God's love for us. From this viewpoint, self-control is not a white-knuckled experience or discipline. It is simply the natural movement of a person who is convinced that God's provision is complete and never failing. Our struggles to find victory over the vices of gluttony, lust, and greed have less to do with the power of their pleasure than with our weak faith in God's love and provision. We use pleasure as a painkiller, because our egos have been weakened and damaged by our distorted vision of God. We see Him as the great killjoy in the sky and not as our Father. We act like greedy and angry consumers rather than grateful, peaceful children. When this conviction and experience reverses, freedom and detachment follow.

### Purity

With an accurate vision and orientation, one that is experiential and not just intellectual, the human person does not have to be bridled. Our interactions with people and things can be natural and free. Our relationships can be characterized by purity and reverence.

C. S. Lewis in his classic *The Weight of Glory* writes, "There are no ordinary people. You have never talked to a mere mortal . . . it is immortals whom we joke with, work with, marry, snub, and exploit."[21] The mystery of God's image extends to every human person. Within each of us there is a "Holy of Holies"—a place where God Himself dwells. Lewis says that our interaction with others "must be of that kind which exists between people who have, from the outset, taken each other seriously—no flippancy, no superiority, no presumption."[22] When this spirit of reverence for the divine mystery in the other takes root in our lives, it produces respect, compassion, and humility. The thought of seeing or using another as an object of self-gratification seems foreign and reprehensible. We can see others for who they really are and not only in relation to ourselves.

This is illustrated by an ancient Christian story retold by Benedicta Ward in her book, *Harlots of the Desert*. A certain Christian bishop named Nonnus was meeting with other bishops in Antioch while a theater troupe passed by them. In the middle of this procession was a beautiful, and scantily clothed, actress named Pelagia. Immediately all the bishops, besides Nonnus, hid their eyes from her by burying their faces in their cloaks. Nonnus, however, was captured by Pelagia's beauty and stared intently at her as she passed. When the troupe was out of sight, Nonnus turned to the other bishops and asked, "Were you not delighted by such great beauty?" Ward comments that "the beauty of Pelagia as a creature formed by God struck Nonnus to the heart; a man of genuine prayer, he was able to see her truly while the more timid men, who were aware of their own capacity for lust, hid their eyes."[23] Vision is everything.

### Charity

When life is viewed as an abundant gift to be cared for and not a possession to be controlled, people and possessions take on a radically different perspective. God has appointed all of us as stewards of these relationships and possessions. We are called to cultivate these good gifts for the purpose of sharing the life and communion of God with others.

Stewardship is fully actualized when we recognize and embrace two things: (1) there is no scarcity in what God provides; and (2) we have earned and deserve nothing except for death but have been given everything good and life-giving by the grace of God. Being convicted of our own spiritual poverty and inspired by gratitude, we can give generously, using our possessions and wealth as tools and resources to work out the love and purposes of God.

Real detachment is rooted in the conviction of God's love and provision. When, through the grace of God's Spirit, our hearts are convinced that God is "Our Father," we no longer become controlled by the changing landscape of life's circumstances and the anxieties they produce. The fact that this broken world offers no real security should cause us no panic, because material security can add nothing to our human identity or destiny. Because of our Father's complete and unconditional love, we are free to live and give like playful children in the moment. It is completely possible to be a *responsible* steward of life's gifts without being poisoned by anxiety—the key is orientation. What is the treasure of your life?

*Peacefulness*

When we are secure in God's love and provision, we live freely. Our identity is not tied to our accomplishments, possessions, or what others think. We aren't easily angered, because we've let go of trying to control people and situations. We are not paralyzed by the voices of the past or the future. Instead we focus on managing our present responses, believing that the providential will of God is revealed in the relationships and circumstances of our everyday life. We ask God to guide our thoughts and feelings, believing that the goodness of God can prevail in the most difficult situations. This confidence fuels a peaceful and stable spirit that is grateful in all things.

When we know we are perfectly loved by God and nothing can be added to or taken away from our identity, we can interact with others without conflict or fear. When we are accused, blamed, and mistreated, we can focus on the other person and not on ourselves. Because we can sense the personal pain and anxiety behind the attack, we are able to respond with compassionate curiosity instead of defensive or offensive words. We are free to love, forgive, and serve the best interests of others. And because we feel free, we are able to bear the fatigue of sacrifice with joy.

### Spiritual Mourning

Our natural response to God's love is expressed through both joy and tears. We will weep when we truly become aware of how much we've been given and all the ways we've squandered those talents and gifts. But at the same time, we will weep for joy over the mercy that has been extended to us despite our brokenness.

This is the bright sadness or joyful sorrow of the heart. It's an orientation and an attitude that reflects the tension and complexity of real life "outside the Garden." When we practice this virtue we have a kind of godly grief that focuses our criticisms on our own actions and produces a spirit of mercy and forgiveness for others. We are eager to come alongside others and cautious about leading, knowing from personal experience that everyone is fiercely tempted until their last dying breath.

Spiritual mourning gives birth to a life-giving humility. It frees us to embrace our struggles, and even our failures, because we know they've been swallowed by the love and Resurrection of Christ. The focus of godly grief is not remorse or regret, but repentance and redemption. This kind of spiritual weeping does not tear away at our identity with personal accusation and judgment, but strengthens it with the affirmation of God's love. These tears can cleanse our souls without weighing them down. They do not end in pity or despair, but in great hope. For this reason, we weep in private but anoint our faces with the oil of joy when in public. We are relieved and energized by the grace of God's forgiveness when we let go of all our defenses and finally embrace who we've become and what we've done. This kind of divine forgiveness only inspires us to extend this grace to others.

### Zeal

If we seek to live a virtuous life, we will refuse to live lives ruined by self-pity or despair. We will place our hope in the goodness and love of God and choose to live our lives zealously focused on obedience. We will spend our energies on translating the love and forgiveness we have received into tangible acts of mercy. And in particular, we will pay special attention to the commands of the Lord to feed the hungry, give drink to the thirsty, show hospitality to the stranger, clothe the naked, and visit the imprisoned. As our lives become less and less consumed with identity and possession, we become freer to spend our resources on the needs of others.

As we mature in the spiritual life, we will also seek to give of ourselves in more complex and vulnerable ways, like instructing the ignorant, encouraging the doubtful, comforting the afflicted, and warning the rebellious. In each of these acts we will patiently bear the weaknesses of those we serve and willingly forgive those who mistreat us. We will no longer choose to act like victims but will make ourselves a living sacrifice to God.

When we are faced with suffering and tribulation, we will not allow ourselves to be overwhelmed with anxiety as though it were unexpected, but we will face the providential will of the Lord with courage, knowing that "all things work together for good to those who love God, to those who are the called according to *His* purpose" (Rom. 8:28). Our zeal will be our joy, and it will inspire others to seek the Lord.

### *Modesty*

Though we are zealous we will be careful to be quiet and hidden. And as much as it is in our power, we will not seek to announce or reveal our good deeds. Since our lives are "hidden with Christ in God" (Col. 3:3), we have no need to supplement our identities with human praise; instead we will seek to be normal human beings.

Modesty is the evidence of a healthy self-understanding. We have love for ourselves without being consumed by self-love. We recognize that we are "fearfully *and* wonderfully made" (Ps. 139:14)—completely unique and incomparable to any other human being. And for this reason, we don't waste our time judging or comparing ourselves to others—it is futile and delusional. We know that each person stands and is judged before God alone.

Modest people are always looking for a way to redeem their

broken identities, not to create new ones. They're not looking to be known for anything special. They only wish to honor God and be faithful to the opportunities for love and obedience on their everyday path.

They know every good fortune in life comes from God, and they are careful never to give the impression they deserved or earned it. They're equally aware that every trial and affliction comes from God as well. In good and bad times they are content and thankful, knowing that their identity and treasure cannot be found in possessions, titles, or human approval. Regardless of their socio-economic standing, modest people seek never to stand out and always share their resources with others.

### Humility

Humility is the beginning and end of all the virtues. It is the evidence that we are not manipulating the people and situations around us to create our own reality. Expressing humility means accepting—and not fighting—life as it comes. It means courageously embracing the life we have, not the one we want. Humility recognizes that human sanctification, not happiness, is the goal of life. This allows us to express our thanksgiving to God even when life is filled with afflictions and sorrows, as it inevitably will be.

The humble person is able to accept that life is a communal experience and that they are not the center of every context. Humble people have a deep dependence on God and recognize that their lives are inextricably bound up with those of their neighbors. These realizations always lead to a life of prayer and service. Humble people don't need to be noticed but are always attentive to the needs of others. They are honest about life and about themselves. They don't seek to edit or justify their personal stories. They are confident in God's redemption and can embrace both the broken and virtuous stories of their lives. When they need help in any area, they seek wise counsel and don't hide from rebuke or direction.

What genuinely sets apart people of humility is their stubborn insistence on living in reality. A life of delusion or fantasy is their greatest fear. They would rather live in real darkness than in false light. They feel this conviction deeply because they believe their present life reveals the sanctifying activity of God's grace.

Because there is no life apart from God, there is no other life than the virtuous one. The virtuous life is reality; every other experience is a distorted shadow of its beauty and truth. The same is true with our identities. Our true selves can only be revealed in the Resurrection of Christ, through our resurrection in and with Him. The life worth living is the life surrendered to God. The pursuit of meaning and identity apart from Christ is insanity and the experience on earth of hell itself. Our lives can only find true significance and fulfillment in the movements, habits, and virtues of the Christian life.

# CHAPTER TEN

# The Final Witness

*You sought us that we might begin to seek you.*

—Augustine

I THOUGHT ABOUT TITLING THIS BOOK *The Tide of God's Love*, because the events of my recent life feel like a tsunami. As I write this book, I'm barely recovering from three devastating years. My ex-wife and I divorced after twenty-two years of marriage, I lost my job and my pastoral vocation, was forced to move away from my three beautiful girls to find work, foreclosed on a house, filed bankruptcy, was forced to say goodbye to a woman I deeply loved, and lost my precious mother to a painful disease. I feel as if my entire existence had been destroyed and swept away in an enormous tide.

After such a catastrophe, in the beginning there is only shock and numbness, the desperate attempt to scramble, gather what you can, and sprint for higher ground. Eventually, however, you realize you can't run fast enough. And when the tsunami catches you, you wonder if you'll survive. There's nothing more primal than the fear of drowning. When I first came up for air,

I could feel the force and weight of my bad decisions crashing and swirling all around me. All I could think about was how bad the subsequent waves were going to be. How was I going to survive? This was all my fault.

But before I could drown in my own self-pity, another shifting force pulled me in the opposite direction. The tide was going out, and the consequences of my decisions and actions felt more scary and devastating than the initial wave of destruction. All around me I could see the shredded and broken pieces of my life, memories, identity, and accomplishments floating into oblivion. To this day, I can't put into words the sheer terror I felt. There is a very real feeling of helplessness—of being dragged out into the middle of the ocean surrounded by the disaster of your life. Will this be the end? Will I drown in the soup of my own brokenness?

"Let not the floodwater overflow me, / Nor let the deep swallow me up" (Ps. 69/70:15), "Stretch out Your hand from above; / Rescue me and deliver me out of great waters" (Ps. 144/145:7). These were the poetic words that ran through my head over and over again. I really wondered if my life was over. But the one thing I never doubted, and still don't, is the love of God. I knew if I were to drown, despite the wreck I'd made of my life, I would somehow drown into the depths of His love. This is the legacy my mother left me and the enduring conviction of my life. God is the Hound of Heaven and pursues all of us with relentless love unto our last, dying breath.

All of us make messes in our lives—it's the human story. The good news is that the final witness of our lives is not the sum total of our bad choices, or even the sum of our good ones. In the end, the final witness is our faith in Christ's love to save us. It's not that our actions don't matter—they do! But it is the work of repentance that illumines every other good work.

Death, then, is the final witness to our lives. It is how we finish the race that matters. All of our lives will be filled with some amount of brokenness and failure, but those who stand back up (resurrect) in the hope of God's mercy and forgiveness will find reward. It's the last breath of our lives that gives witness to every other breath we've taken. If our last breath is taken with humility and faith in God's undying love, we will find salvation and our true destiny as human beings.

I have always said that the greatest blessing of being a pastor was the time I spent at the bedsides of the dying. That may sound morbid, but my life has been deeply enriched by the clarity that has come from spending time with these people. In these contexts, there is rarely any talk of work, money, accomplishments, or ego. Dying people want to talk about relationships—their relationship with God and those to whom they feel closest. Their emotions and thoughts reflect the joys and anxieties they experience in these relationships. At the end of life, relational security is their greatest treasure and the only thing they can take with them. Many people hold on for an opportunity to make even the smallest of gestures to resolve the pain and uncertainty of their relational history. All of us come into this world with a natural orientation and movement toward others, and despite how we lived, all of us leave this world with an intuitive understanding of the value of relationships. At death, it's our relationships, including our relationship with God, that witness and validate the worth of our good works.

Our lives are not over yet. Our final testimony has not yet been recorded. Death is the true and final witness. Our faithlessness and betrayals are swallowed by the ocean of God's love. We do not have to fear our pasts, our brokenness, and our secrets; we can embrace all of them with honesty, knowing that we are loved, forgiven, and empowered to live differently. We are children of the resurrection. When we fall down, we stand back up, reorient, and keep going. We are learning to be grateful and to act hopeful despite our thoughts and feelings. Above all, we know that God is always doing everything in His mighty power to save us and to demonstrate His love for us.

The Christian musician John Michael Talbot wrote a touching song entitled "Shepherd Boy." The song tells the story of a young boy whose love for a shepherd girl leaves his heart broken and wounded. His pain, however, is not in the wound, but in the fact that she has forgotten him. This "one thought" causes the young shepherd boy so much pain that he follows her into a distant land, and, to search for her, climbs up "Love's tree," where he spreads his arms in an eternal gesture of love and dies.

On that great day when "all nations, tribes, peoples, and tongues [is gathered] before the throne and before the Lamb" (Rev. 7:9), and while the angels sing, "Holy, holy, holy, / Lord God Almighty" (Rev. 4:8), a voice from heaven will be heard saying, "the marriage of the Lamb has come . . . Blessed *are* those who are called to the marriage supper of the Lamb" (Rev. 19:7, 9). The groom will enter the feast on a white charger, wearing a victor's crown and clothed in a robe dipped in love's blood. His eyes will be bright "like a flame of fire" (Rev. 19:12). And when His eyes meet yours, it will all become perfectly clear. It is *you* He has come for. It is *you* whom He has always loved.

In this eternal moment, everything in your life will make sense—every moment, every relationship, every pain, every joy. Your entire being will combust in recognition that you were made for Him. And with this recognition, you will fall to your knees in wonder and disbelief of such unfathomable love. All those prodigal years you ran after other loves, He never stopped pursuing you.

Like a tender father, He will reach down and wipe away every tear of remorse and regret from your eyes. The warmth of His irresistible love will remove the sorrows and pains of your heart. Instinctively, you will reach out for Him. And as His nail-scarred hand grabs your limp and helpless wrist and raises you to your feet, your mind will race to every feeble and half-baked effort of repentance and virtue you've ever attempted. You know that all your "righteousnesses *are* like filthy rags" (Is. 64:6), and they amount to nothing. The only thing they reveal is desire. You want to be saved. You want to say "yes" to Him.

With this awareness, it will finally dawn on you: the entire vocation of man is to reach out in desire toward the Creator and say "yes" to His love. Standing in front of Him, completely resurrected, you will hear the words that every fiber in your being has longed to hear since the day you took your first breath: "Well *done*, good and faithful servant; you have been faithful over a few things . . . Enter into the joy of your lord" (Matt. 25:23).

# Notes

1 C.S. Lewis, *Mere Christianity* (San Francisco: HarperCollins, 2009), p. 136.

2 Elizabeth Barrett Browning, *Aurora Leigh: A Poem in Nine Books* (T. Y. Crowell & Co., 1883), p. 265.

3 Michael Guillen, *Can a Smart Person Believe in God?* (2004), p. 90.

4 C. G. Jung, trans. H. G. Baynes & C. F. Baynes, *Contributions to Analytical Psychology* (Routledge & Kegan Paul, 1948), p. 193.

5 George MacDonald, *Unspoken Sermons:* Series I, II, III (Nuvision Publications, 2007), p. 260.

6 Melissa Giovagnoli, *Angels in the workplace: stories and inspirations for creating a new world of work* (Jossey-Bass, 1999).

7 Frederica Mathewes-Green, "The Wounded Torturer," *In Communion*, summer issue 2007/ IC 46.

8 St. Isaac the Syrian, homily 68, *The Ascetical Homilies.*

9 John Ortberg, *The Life You've always Wanted: Spiritual Disciplines for Ordinary People* (Zondervan, 2002), p. 11.

10 "God Is Always With You," interview with Father Roman Braga by Jessica Precop, http://wonder.oca.org/2012/05/29/god-is-always-with-you-an-interview-with-father-roman-braga/

11 Ibid.

12 *Testimonies About Faith* (video), http://www.pbs.org/wgbh/pages/frontline/shows/pope/testimony/

13 Timothy Keller, *The Reason for God: Belief in an Age of Skepticism* (Viking, 2008), p. 54.

14 Daphne Rae, *Love Until It Hurts* (HarperCollins, 1981).

15 Compiled and Edited by Charles E. Moore, *Provocations: Spiritual Writings of Kierkegaard* (The Bruderhof Foundation, Inc., 2002), p. 201.

15 *Autobiography of a Saint,* translated by Ronald Knox (Collins, 1973), p. 44.

17 Matthew A. Killingsworth, Daniel T. Gilbert, " A Wandering Mind Is an Unhappy Mind," *Science*, 12 Nov 2010: Vol. 330, Issue 6006, p. 932.

18 Father Roman Braga, *Exploring the Inner Universe: Joy, the Mystery of Life* (Holy Dormition Monastery Press, 1996), p. 125.

19 Rumi, "The Guest House," *Rumi: The Book of Love*, trans. and commentary by Coleman Barks (New York: HarperCollins, 2003), pp. 179–180.

20 As quoted in https://www.psychologytoday.com/blog/evolution-the-self/201606/you-only-get-more-what-you-resist-why

21 C.S. Lewis, "The Weight of Glory," preached originally as a sermon in the Church of St Mary the Virgin, Oxford, on June 8, 1942; published in THEOLOGY, November, 1941, and by the S.P.C.K, 1942, p. 9.

22 Ibid.

23 From *The Life of St. Pelagia the Harlot* (*Vita Sanctae Pelagiae, Meretricis*), translated by Sr. Benedicta Ward, S.L.G., "Pelagia, Beauty Riding By," in *Harlots of the Desert: A study of repentance in early monastic sources* (Cistercian Publications, Inc., Kalamazoo, 1986): Latin Text in PL 73, 663–672.

KEVIN SCHERER is a writer and speaker with twenty years of pastoral counseling experience. As a former evangelical pastor and Eastern Orthodox priest, he has pastored in seven churches and served as the executive director of two nationwide Christian ministries. He also served as a chaplain at Ground Zero following the events of 9/11 as well as the Virginia Tech and Northern Illinois University shootings. Based on these personal experiences, two degrees in theology, and his own personal challenges, Kevin has developed an intuition for coming alongside people in the most difficult and confusing moments of their lives. He is remarried, the father of five girls, and currently lives in Northwest Arkansas.

**Becoming a Healing Presence**
*by Albert S. Rossi, PhD*

In order to become a healing presence for others, we must first be healed ourselves—through an active relationship with the great Healer, Christ. Drawing on the teachings of the Fathers and saints of the Church, Dr. Rossi gently points the way toward deepening our love for God and for each other so that others may experience Christ through us.

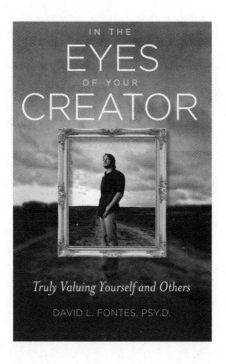

**In the Eyes of Your Creator:**
**Truly Valuing Yourself and Others**
*by David L. Fontes, Psy.D.*

Many of the ills of our society can be traced to the sense of worthlessness that afflicts so many people today. If we only understood in the depths of our being how valuable we are in the eyes of our Creator, we could learn to obey Christ's commandment to love our neighbor as ourselves. Priest and counselor David Fontes marries the best insights of psychology with those of the spiritual tradition of the Orthodox Church to point the way toward this understanding.

Ancient Faith Publishing hopes you have enjoyed and benefited from this book. The proceeds from the sales of our books only partially cover the costs of operating our nonprofit ministry—which includes both the work of **Ancient Faith Publishing** and the work of **Ancient Faith Radio**. Your financial support makes it possible to continue this ministry both in print and online. Donations are tax-deductible and can be made at **www. ancientfaith.com**.

To request a catalog of other publications,
please call us at (800) 967-7377 or (219) 728-2216
or log onto our website: **store.ancientfaith.com**

Bringing you Orthodox Christian music, readings,
prayers, teaching, and podcasts 24 hours a day since 2004 at
**www.ancientfaith.com**